CUTTING-EDGE IDEAS
EMPOWERING AGENTS OF POSITIVE WORLD CHANGE

LAURA FIENOR

First Edition
Published in Boorloo [Perth, Australia] by Laura Fienor Fields, 2024
lfiel@live.com.au

Copyright © Laura Fienor Fields, 2024

All rights reserved

A catalogue record for this work is available
from the National Library of Australia

Author:	Fienor, Laura 1973-.
Title:	Cutting-edge ideas: empowering agents of positive world change / by Laura Fienor.
ISBN:	9780994304872 (pbk).
Notes:	Bibliography.
Subjects:	Educational theory. Legal theory. Psychological theory. World philosophies.

Cover Photography:
Front: 'Connectedness' by JMMN (Instagram: jose_viajero_)
Back: 'Exmouth' by JMMN (Instagram: jose_viajero_)

FOR ALL ENQUIRIES REGARDING THIS BOOK, CONTACT THE PUBLISHER AT:

lfiel@live.com.au

*Everything you do has an impact -
in the moment; across a lifetime; and into Infinity.*

PREFACE

The aim of this book is to provide motivated citizens with a range of innovative ideas that will help empower them to become agents of positive world change. Please note that the text contains information drawn from a wide range of theoretical perspectives. Documenting ideas from many different fields of inquiry (including Futures Studies; Education; Law; Environmental Science; Psychology; Neuroscience; Philosophy; Spirituality; Quantum Physics; Indigenous Knowledges; and New Age, Metaphysical, Mystical, and Esoteric Studies) means that there may be some ideologies which are contradictory in nature. Given that the concern of this publication is to present a large number of different (and perhaps quite divergent) 'cutting-edge ideas', it will not seek to resolve any apparent inconsistencies in the approaches being presented (especially since some of the material is still being developed, and written or theorised about, in quite 'new' ways for Western minds). Even if readers are sceptical about some of the ideas, there may still be key concepts that prove to be useful in the personal empowerment process, and which will ultimately assist individuals in working to create a better world. When evaluating the various strategies, it is important to keep an open mind and find commonalities and unity in diverse beliefs (especially if they are able to bring great benefit to the world). It is also worth noting that many scientists are increasingly relying on explanations for phenomena that they cannot prove in standardised ways, and 'subjective truth', 'uncertainty', and 'unpredictability' are now dominant notions in many academic disciplines.

If some approaches do not fit within one's personal 'comfort zone', then it is nonetheless important to maintain a level of respect and not promote division between humans working collectively towards the greater goal of creating a better world. Intelligent conversations and direct debates should always be favoured over simplistic and negative social media commentaries (which often feature unresearched assumptions and claims of a demonstrably false nature). Sources that contain detailed bibliographies can usually be regarded as favouring more reliable and trustworthy information - or at least material which is worth additional consideration and deeper investigation. As with all areas of study, the individual should delve further into those ideas which most resonate with them.

CONTENTS

PREFACE *i*

INTRODUCTION: An Overview of Contemporary World Problems + The Dominant Ideologies and Education System Practices That Fostered Their Generation *v*

PART 1: Cutting-Edge Ideas Relating to Education System Transformation *1*
Chapter 1: Futures-Based Transformations for More Relevant, Engaging, and Ethical Education *3*
Chapter 2: A Transitionary Education Model That Aims To Generate a Preferable Future for Humanity and the Environment *13*
Chapter 3: Indigenous Education Model *27*
Chapter 4: Proposed Legal Action for Education System Transformation *39*

PART 2: Empowering Agents of Positive World Change Through Key Processes, Concepts, Guidance, and Insights *45*
Chapter 5: Empowering Agents of Positive World Change Through Life Purpose Establishment / Clarification Processes *47*
Chapter 6: Empowering Agents of Positive World Change Through Multidisciplinary Conceptions of 'Infinity' and 'Unity' *53*
Chapter 7: Empowering Agents of Positive World Change Through Various Forms of Guidance *63*
Chapter 8: Empowering Agents of Positive World Change Through Various Forms of Insight *81*

PART 3: Empowering Agents of Positive World Change Through Practical Well-Being Activities *97*
Chapter 9: Physical Well-Being Activities *99*
Chapter 10: Mental Well-Being Activities *109*
Chapter 11: Emotional Well-Being Activities *119*

APPENDICES   *129*
Appendix A: Insight Into The Spiritual Relationship Between Native Americans and Nature   *131*
Appendix B: Infinity as a Universal and Unifying Concept   *133*
Appendix C: Dietary Guidelines   *151*
Appendix D: The Physical, Psychological, and Social Effects of Substance Use and Abuse   *153*
Appendix E: Strategies for Clearing Negative Energies   *157*

BIBLIOGRAPHY   *159*

RECOMMENDED SOURCES   *174*

ACKNOWLEDGEMENT

This book was written on Turrbal, Kaurna, and Whadjuk Noongar lands. The author wishes to acknowledge that no Aboriginal peoples of the land currently known as Australia have ever been provided with the opportunity to sign a Treaty, either with the original British invaders of the land, or with the non-Indigenous peoples who are continuing to occupy Country. The author recognises that her daily practices have continuing and far-reaching cultural consequences of a problematic nature for all Indigenous peoples, as well as serious environmental impacts that have detrimental implications at both local and global levels. She hopes that there will increasingly be a global revitalisation of traditional Indigenous ideologies, knowledges, and practices as humanity evolves to greater spiritual awareness, cultural integrity, and environmental sustainability.

INTRODUCTION

AN OVERVIEW OF CONTEMPORARY WORLD PROBLEMS

+

THE DOMINANT IDEOLOGIES AND EDUCATION SYSTEM PRACTICES THAT FOSTERED THEIR GENERATION

Introduction
- An Overview of Contemporary World Problems
- How Dominant Schooling Curricula Generate Global Problems
- The Trend of Environmental Devastation
- The Ideologies and Education System Practices Generating Environmental Devastation
- The Trends of Social Inequity and Injustice
- The Ideologies and Education System Practices Generating Social Inequities and Injustice
- The Trends of Violence and War
- The Ideologies and Education System Practices Generating Violence and War
- The Trends of Psychological, Physical, and Spiritual Dysfunction
- The Ideologies and Education System Practices Generating Personal Dysfunction
- Other Underlying Issues

> *Readers who already have a high level of awareness of the key existential, moral, and well-being issues facing humanity (and the dominant ideologies and education system practices that have given rise to them), may prefer to go straight to the more optimistic and action-oriented parts of this book. While it is important to be realistic and deeply aware of the scale of global concerns currently facing humanity, it is also essential to stay motivated; focus on meaningful action; and maintain a sense of hope while being committed to generating positive world change.

An Overview of Contemporary World Problems

As a result of the harm to the environment and wider humanity currently being caused by inequitable and unjust social systems that are becoming increasingly dominant on a global scale, unprecedented existential threats and forms of suffering are being generated for all landscapes, animals, and peoples. While International legal systems continue to fail in their duty to develop and enforce laws that protect entire ecological systems and animal species from annihilation and extinction, high-polluting world citizens must immediately take it upon themselves to transform how they survive (and how they learn to survive) on a grossly over-populated and resource-scarce planet. Since violence and ecocide are system-wide problems, and because peoples in money-based countries are still using schools to *teach* their children how to massively exploit resources and over-consume to 'survive', blaming the planet's woes solely on politicians (who the masses voted into power) and corporations (who the masses buy from) is having minimal impact on healing and saving the world. The damaging actions of all individuals affiliated with harm-creating institutions and systems must, then, be transformed if ecologically destructive, socially unjust, and inherently violent ideologies and practices are to be eliminated.

How Dominant Schooling Curricula Generate Global Problems

In its current form, the Western education system works powerfully to perpetuate inequity, conflict, and environmental degradation – that is, to create, rather than resolve, a myriad of global problems. Schools dominated by industrial-military knowledge are increasingly imposed on the globalised masses in an attempt to perpetuate a serious problem-creating status quo. As such, for the dominant education system to play a transformative role, it cannot take the traditional forms of academic rationalism or social adaptation. The former approach divides knowledge into discrete disciplines and often focuses on abstract academic concepts that both cause, and are divorced from realistic solutions to, global problems. Such knowledge has been used to maintain positions of dominance and subjugation within social, political, and economic structures, as well as large-scale ecological abuse in the name of Industrial Era 'development'.

The Trend of Environmental Devastation

Countries with large money-based economies are responsible for the post-1945 levels of consumption and associated carbon emissions that are causing climate change. High-polluting peoples are also generating unprecedented levels of environmental devastation – harm to nature so extreme that the most common future prediction being made by knowledgeable climatologists, ecologists, and geologists is that all species (including humans) are facing imminent mass extinction. In *Deep Green Resistance: Strategy to Save the Planet,* Lierre Keith says that we are already living in a period of mass extinction (the first one caused by humans alone). Of additional concern is that resources and labour in economically disadvantaged countries are being increasingly exploited to feed the rampant consumerism of wealthier nations.

While previous centuries were characterised by the overt imperial expansion of European powers and their exploitation (and alteration) of each colony's natural resources, the cultural imperialism occurring now is far more insidious, as the globalising of Western ideologies (like capitalism and materialism) and practices (such as the use of technology to dominate and destroy nature for profit) is resulting in the environment being devastated more rapidly and in a larger number of locations throughout the world. Evidence for the trend of significant and widespread ecological degradation is voluminous. According to the *Global Stewards* website, humanity must immediately find solutions to a very wide range of environmental problems, including air and water pollution from toxic chemicals; forest and habitat destruction (leading to more endangered species and biodiversity loss); climate change; desertification; and shrinking wetlands. Such threats to nature have already resulted in a range of negative outcomes for the planet and its peoples (especially those from Indigenous backgrounds). Various Native American peoples have repeatedly emphasised the fact that while they live in harmony with the Earth and its rhythms, Westerners have persistently engaged in acts of exploitation – utilising commercial and industrial practices to generate profit whilst poisoning land, water, and air (as well as the creatures dependent on them), and thereby threatening the oneness of the planet.

By employing foresight (such as through trend extrapolation), it is possible to project that a range of additional survival-threatening consequences will emerge if such trends are to continue. Climate destabilisation has already resulted in rising sea levels and increasing global temperatures; deforestation has caused the planet to lose the majority of its forest cover, with topsoil being eroded faster than it can be recreated as a result of the spread of intensive agricultural practices; oceans are acidifying, coral reefs dying, and phytoplankton populations collapsing because of the dumping of multiple toxins into the sea and waterways by various corporations; and mass extinctions are occurring on an unprecedented scale due to widespread industrial activity (with more than half of all species currently threatened). Clearly then, unless currently-observable trends like resource over-use and ecological abuse are halted, a more dystopian future will be in store for humankind.

The Ideologies and Education System Practices Generating Environmental Devastation

In engaging in detailed critiques of the ideologies that underpin ecologically harmful practices, many environmentalists and futurists are highly critical of the belief systems that have characterised industrialised and consumerist societies – nature as an unlimited resource that can be polluted and used to generate wealth; excessive materialism and greed as being highly desirable qualities; and individualistic and competitive behaviours being the favourable methods for attaining increased power and salaries in corporations that disregard the environmental consequences of their business activities. Essentially, the most serious problems in the contemporary world have arisen because of the success of the Industrial society paradigm. Worldwide environmental destruction, resource depletion, and the increasing collapse of life-supporting ecological systems are the consequences of money-based ideologies and practices that are creating problems faster than they can solve them – they are also all interconnected parts of a single world problem at the macrocosmic level. Another dimension of the issue is that many financially advantaged peoples do not actually want to adopt a sustainable way of life – they actively want to maintain a functionally unsustainable civilisation. Refusals to sacrifice financial wealth, personal status, and narcissistic practices can undoubtedly be blamed for widespread ecocide and the pending omnicide (that is, total extinction of the human species as a result of human action).

It is also clear that formal educational institutions feature organisational structures, curricula, and pedagogical practices that work to reinforce nature-threatening ideologies. For instance, the dominance of rationalism in academic curricula has frequently led to the development of knowledge that is free from ethical concerns, and to justify extensive ecological abuse in the name of Industrial Era 'growth' and 'progress'. As well, the dominant curricula delivered in contemporary schools across the world causes significant long-term ideological harm to young people, as it teaches them how to engage in extreme acts of environmental destruction, heavy technology dependency, and grossly inequitable forms of hierarchy-based status achievement. Indeed, students of all cultural and racial backgrounds now learn deeply problematic forms of knowledge via subjects like Business (with an emphasis on maximising monetary profit – even at the expense of nature); Technology (focused on using human-made products to defy the natural world); Science (which is increasingly moving away from mere observation and towards active interference with nature in artificial and environmentally dangerous ways); Physical Education (via the teaching of competitive forms of physical activity, including all types of sport, which are at philosophical odds with the cooperative practices of many traditional Eastern and Indigenous peoples); and Economics (through studying industrial-society monetary systems rather than ecologically-friendly forms of survival like gathering and hunting or permaculture). Units delivered in various Arts, Social Sciences, and Humanities subjects are also excessively Anglo- or Eurocentric in nature. For instance, the study of mass-produced and mass-circulated Shakespearean plays is now foregrounded over local storytelling practices in many countries across the world. This means that Indigenous Elders are no longer provided with the right to sit, daily, with the young to ensure that they are cared for in an holistic way and are able to hear the myths and legends which will motivate them to look after country in an appropriate manner. Instead, pupils are exposed to a highly homogenised form of education in line with mass-produced government documents like syllabuses. As such, the world now produces millions of individuals who go on to destroy vastly wiser and more valuable Indigenous cultures whilst actively exploiting the environment (this, in turn, generates growing physical harm for all humans through pollution and extreme weather events). Thus, educational curricula as they are currently constituted actually support the industrial and technological way of life that is creating the world's most serious problems. By critiquing the dominant ideologies of those societies that continue to foreground money-based materialism, it would be possible to advocate for the adoption of less ecologically-hazardous educational and social practices.

The Trends of Social Inequity and Injustice

Humans across the globe are made unequal by the significant distinctions that exist in levels of wealth, status, political power, cultural autonomy, and / or military capacity, as well as access to land, material goods, or the basic resources necessary for survival. Western-educated peoples are especially responsible for extreme forms of social injustice generated by the perpetuation of inequitable hierarchies, as well as a constant emphasis on status, the hoarding of money, and the exploitation of other lands and peoples for maximum profit. In such a society, the ideologies and practices of individualism and competition are favoured over cooperation, collaboration, and connectedness. The negative implications of entrenched inequities are many and varied – from the eruption of wars and acts of genocide, to the emergence of poverty-stricken ghettos, in which drug and alcohol abuse are commonly resorted to in an effort to escape the realities of social disadvantage. The economic and political ideologies and practices of money-based countries thus create cycles of poverty, as well as wider feelings of pessimism and nihilism. Culturally biased legal systems then exacerbate social divisions by disproportionately targeting already-disadvantaged peoples for 'low-level crimes', while 'white collar crimes' are extensively ignored (including financial sector fraud, politicians' travel rorts, and casino money laundering). Punitive approaches to key minority populations (for instance, juveniles from certain socioeconomic backgrounds) frequently result in recidivism rather than crime elimination.

The globalisation of capitalist activities also means that extreme injustice is increasingly occurring across nations, as those in wealthy nations further maximise exploitation of labour and resources in economically disadvantaged regions of the world. Indeed, the planet's rapid population growth since the 1800s and the more recent drought / desertification caused by climate change (generated by high-polluting rich peoples engaged in rampant consumerism), means that the total number of people facing malnutrition, famine, starvation and / or thirst (through inadequate access to fresh food and clean water) or other survival-threatening forms of squalor is indeed growing. At the time of the publication of this book, it is reported that the world's richest 1% own more than 45% of the world's wealth, while over 52% of the world's population own little more than 1% of the world's wealth. The rich are indeed getting richer while over 700 million people face extreme poverty and hunger. As such, the trend of growing inequality between people of different classes, cultures, and races is something which humanity must seek to halt in order to avoid a more dystopian future.

The Ideologies and Education System Practices Generating Social Inequities and Injustice

In most contemporary societies, divisions occur through a defined system of class structure, based on inequitable distributions of money, power, and resources. Such stratification is often determined in schools, where minorities are deliberately discriminated against through fundamentally biased processes of assessment, grading, and ranking. For instance, because the knowledge of middle- and upper-class people is valued, taught, and assessed, those peoples who possess different bodies of knowledge are consistently labelled as 'low' or 'very low' achievers. Long-standing beliefs in 'genetic inequality' still underpin educational systems and work to maintain the kind of (unofficial) class structures that foster discrimination against the poor and certain minorities. The dominant education system also works powerfully to perpetuate social injustices by treating students as potential forms of 'human capital' who will eventually serve to keep wider capitalist society functioning with all its inherent inequities. Educators thus invariably become agents of social reproduction – indoctrinating students in such a way as to perpetuate a status quo that rests on inequitable class structures. As such, teachers are actually a powerful force of intellectual and social control, pressuring students to be obedient and using standardised tests to hierarchically sort them for a society that primarily values monetary and material 'success'. The hidden curriculum in schools is also characterised by racism, sexism, and socioeconomic inequities, while educators continue to focus on trivial matters (like whether students are wearing the 'correct' uniform or not). Indeed, institutions which offer technical courses are implicitly accepting the status quo, providing students with a socially adaptive rather than empowering education that will usually end in them moving into the low status and minimum wage jobs that offer few decision-making powers. The fact that students from Indigenous, minority, and low socioeconomic backgrounds are the ones most likely to be streamed into vocational subjects means that wider society subsequently becomes characterised by inequities in access to power and wealth according, primarily, to issues of race or pre-existing financial position – with crime and violence often then resulting from such unequal relations.

Another common criticism of the dominant education system is that it preferences middle-class values, content, and teaching and assessment methods, while pupils from Indigenous, multicultural, and low socioeconomic backgrounds are the ones most likely to be disadvantaged by the schooling process. The very act of putting traditionally-oriented Indigenous pupils into school buildings (thereby removing them from the natural environment) and asking them to study Western forms of numeracy, science, and literacy (all delivered in an invading language) is a highly imperialistic act and inevitably results in complete student disengagement in many instances. Also causing great ideological harm in schools is the fact that many teachers show complete ignorance of traditional Indigenous methods of education, in which all forms of knowledge are integrated according to a spiritually-based care for the environment (that is, knowledge and action are always considered in an holistic manner rather than as discrete parts of artificially defined 'subject areas' that regard nature as separate and controllable). As well, cooperative styles of learning are frequently overridden by competitive and hierarchical methods, and a much wider form of cultural genocide is occurring when Indigenous oral and visual knowledges are usurped by written literacy practices.

Teachers further ideologically harm children through the use of artificial forms of pedagogy that are restricted to classroom (rather than natural) settings, and standardised assessment instruments that aim to rank the students as forms of human capital. Essentially, dominant evaluation and grading practices cause students to be constantly stressed via an endless series of tests and assignments; competitive rather than cooperative with their peers; and more obsessed with personal career advancement and wealth accumulation than with achieving personal well-being or globally-beneficial forms of sustainability, peace, and equity. Feelings of self-worth and being a valued member of society therefore become psychologically enmeshed in the testing situation, contributing further to student distress and the destructive sense of being judged. Indeed, countless children suffer from lifelong psychological harm as a result of being widely labelled as 'low' or 'very low achievers' (Ds and Es) because they are not culturally suited for engagement in the environmentally-destructive capitalist practices of Western society. Also causing untold damage is the use of bell curves to determine exit scores and, therefore, which predominantly middle- and upper-class children will be granted privileged access to university (so that they can go on to enjoy the most high-status and high-power jobs post-graduation), and which predominantly low socioeconomic children will become the less empowered labourers. Setting up key sectors of society for a lifetime of disadvantage then generates entrenched divisions and serious society-wide problems.

When teachers impose socially dominant belief systems on culturally diverse peoples, they are not in any way meeting students' pastoral needs, but are actually generating extreme and very serious forms of emotional harm. Indeed, large numbers of Indigenous peoples worldwide suffer from ideological confusion, loss of identity, and mental health issues because they are consistently categorised as 'failures' by an education system that repeatedly judges and labels them in a negative way for not thinking in accordance with the dominant culture. Ultimately, then, it is clear that educational institutions need, themselves, to be critiqued, and the curriculum they offer must truly (not just rhetorically) cater to the diversity of all student bodies.

The Trends of Violence and War

Western countries have engaged in more large-scale mass killings using 'sophisticated' forms of technological weaponry than any other peoples on the planet. Indeed, more lives were lost as a result of the technology-heavy wars of the Twentieth Century than at any other time in human history. Despite this fact, contemporary peoples continue to justify war in annual ceremonies and through emotionally simplistic moralism and nationalism. The reality is that most dominant and wealthy world powers have engaged, for centuries, in acts of armed take-over, the genocide of native peoples, and the rape of environments all over the planet. For example, it is well known that at one stage the British Empire covered a quarter of the globe, while most other Western European countries have also had dozens of colonial interests in every part of the world (from Africa and Asia to the Pacific and the Americas). In fact, key nations (which now regularly denounce the violence of other states) are still living off the wealth earned through their participation in multiple forms of exploitation and terror against the resources and peoples of poor, small, and Indigenous countries. Successive leaders of many Western countries have also failed to note that they are part of an ongoing illegal and violent invasion of First Nations lands (for example, no Treaty having ever been signed with Aboriginal Australians to relieve them of such a status), with multiple acts of terror against the environment (including habitat destruction, species genocide, and extreme pollution) and harm to Indigenous peoples continuing on unabated. As such, colonial invasions; massacres of foreign citizens; war via military dominance over a country with smaller weapons capacity; and capitalist-style exploitation of resources and workers in 'undeveloped' regions are all examples of the violent practices that continue to underpin conflict on a global scale.

With the growing dominance of technology in global society, it is also clear that the human 'intellect' has been responsible for inventing machines that now provide all people with the extremely serious threat of complete annihilation by Artificial Intelligence (AI). While humans choose to celebrate (rather than critique) their own supposed 'cleverness' and technological inventions, then wholesale elimination of the species will continue to loom large. Ultimately, it is the high levels of technology and weaponry enabled by countries with money-based economies that is posing the greatest threat to humanity's survival and peace.

The Ideologies and Education System Practices Generating Violence and War

It is in formal educational institutions that many contemporary peoples learn the ideologies which prompt them to engage in acts of low-level violence against individuals known to them, as well as to establish unequal relations *across* nations. Indeed, schools are structured in an hierarchical manner (with those in positions of authority frequently engaging in acts of bullying against those of lesser power), and they repeatedly focus on promoting competition and achievement at the expense of others (through processes of testing, grading, and ranking). Via constant exposure to such practices, young people then come to embrace the dominant philosophies of power and materialism (individualism and personal greed) and so grow up to accept the 'necessity' of violence against other peoples in order for the exploitation of resources to continue on unabated (that is, so that their unending addiction to consumerism, via such commodities as oil, can be perpetually met).

It is interesting to note that no traditional-living Indigenous peoples can be credited with the invention of guns, atomic bombs, drones, or devastating chemical agents, as cooperation for survival was more extensively focused on in holistic forms of education (where responsibilities to the land and its creatures were emphasised over dominating nature with the technology-based inventions of science). In Australia, the myths and legends of Aboriginal peoples also show no evidence of participation in large-scale international wars or illegal and violent invasions of other countries (or the enslavement, assimilation, and continued genocide of foreign peoples and their cultures). Instead, peace and harmony with neighbouring kinship clans was consistently maintained through methods of intermarriage and the ideological belief that 'all are connected and all are one'.

The Trends of Psychological, Physical, and Spiritual Dysfunction

With the global spread of a spiritually disconnected society that is dominated by technology and consumerism, millions of contemporary peoples are facing increasing forms of stress, anxiety, angst, and obesity. Recent studies have also shown that many users of social media sites are suffering from depression – some theories being that individuals develop low self-esteem if they constantly view others seemingly having a 'better life' than they are, and that the act of documenting the minutiae of one's everyday life online leads to a very psychologically unhealthy form of narcissism and self-absorption. Indeed, many individuals are now obsessing more about updating (and often falsely manipulating) their own digital profile than the emotionally healthy pursuit of helping others. Some psychologists also claim that the (frequently negative or bullying) attention generated by the posting of personal photos and details on the worldwide web is akin to having experienced a traumatic event. Ultimately, while so many contemporary peoples actively disrespect nature in their pursuit of shallow forms of greed and over-consumption of technological products, it seems inevitable that rates of psychological, emotional, physical, and spiritual dysfunction will continue to rise.

The Ideologies and Education System Practices Generating Personal Dysfunction

The dominant education system, with its heavy focus on abstract rationalism (rather than nature-bound spirituality), is deeply unholistic in character and occurs in artificial classroom settings where the young are required to sit for extended periods of time (in physically unhealthy ways) and are often bullied into submission, regardless of their individual psychological and emotional needs. Schools also seem to be almost exclusively dedicated to making students functionally literate and numerate – that is, as forms of unquestioning and uncritical human capital who will become obedient workers and consumers. Meanwhile, lessons in human relationships are widely regarded as tokenistic in nature (a way to 'fill in' timetables), while the bulk of the serious emphasis is increasingly on how students perform on standardised tests - that is, centrally devised assessments which do not in any way evaluate the wisdom, mental and emotional well-being, or spiritual and ethical integrity of the pupils.

Traditional-living Indigenous peoples across the world claim that, prior to Western invasion, they lived long, physically and mentally healthy lives - with nutritious diets; large amounts of regular walking; emotionally supportive and cooperative communities; and strong spiritual ties to the natural world all being provided as reasons for their holistic well-being. As such, money-based societies that have an entrenched dependence on the ideologies of individualism and competition need to deeply transform their education institutions and entire social structures if increasing forms of personal dysfunction are to be successfully stemmed.

Other Underlying Issues

The social systems that are currently dominant in the world seem to be generating more problems than they are solving. Concerned citizens frequently report large levels of bureaucratic self-justification, denial, and inertia when complaints are lodged or legitimate issues are raised. Of further concern is that politicians frequently publicly attack each other on multiple matters rather than respectfully collaborating to solve global problems. Large amounts of time, energy, and effort are also expended on reactive policies that pander to shallow agendas as a result of short electoral cycles. Indeed, long-term planetary needs are repeatedly ignored in favour of less important matters that dominant media outlets work to popularise. While readers are considering the material in this book, they may like to formulate answers to the following questions:
1. How can humanity make social systems serve the greater global good rather than generate more global problems?
2. Can one system be effectively used to hold another system to account or transform it? For example, can the legal system be used to alter the education system? Does humanity have enough time to engage in protracted legal cases?
3. What forms of cultural transformation would be most effective?

PART 1:
CUTTING-EDGE IDEAS RELATING TO EDUCATION SYSTEM TRANSFORMATION

Chapter 1: Futures-Based Transformations for More Relevant, Engaging, and Ethical Education
- Creating Eutopian Alternatives Through Education System Transformation
- The Purpose of Futures-Based Education System Transformation
- The Lack of Contemporary Relevance of Dominant Schooling Curricula and Practices
- Ways to Transform Curriculum
- Ways to Transform Methods of Evaluation and Pedagogy
- A Journey of Hope, Action, and Transformation

Chapter 2: A Transitionary Education Model That Aims to Generate a Preferable Future for Humanity and the Environment
- Proposed Curriculum, Pedagogy, and Evaluation Programme That Incorporates Futures-Based Educational Theory and Caters To Western, Indigenous, Holistic, and Multicultural Knowledges
- The Productive Pedagogies
- 'Shaping a Better Future' Project Ideas for the Sustainability and Environmental Stewardship Theme
- 'Shaping a Better Future' Project Ideas for the Global Peace and Harmony Theme
- 'Shaping a Better Future' Project Ideas for the Equity and Social Justice in Multicultural Societies Theme
- 'Shaping a Better Future' Project Ideas for the Body, Mind, and Soul Matters Theme
- Futures-Based 'Create a Better World' Community Planning Ideas
- Ways to Implement Futures Studies

Chapter 3: Indigenous Education Model
- Australian Aboriginal Knowledges of Spiritual and Practical Benefit to Contemporary Peoples
- The Benefits of an Indigenous Education Model
- Australian Aboriginal Ideologies Regarding Natural Environments
- Australian Aboriginal Educational Approaches in Relation to Natural Environments
- Australian Aboriginal Ideologies Regarding Equity and Peace
- Australian Aboriginal Educational Approaches in Promoting Peace and Equity
- Summary of the Environmental and Social Benefits of Dominant Australian Aboriginal Ideologies and Practices
- Comparative Chart: Western / Global Society Problems – Aboriginal Society Solutions

Chapter 4: Proposed Legal Action for Education System Transformation
- Potential Legal Cases to Force Education System Transformation
- Parens Patriae and Duty of Person Who Has Care of Child
- Abuse of Office and Refusal by Public Officer to Perform Duty
- Neglect and Educational Negligence / Malpractice
- Other Legal Options

CHAPTER 1
FUTURES-BASED TRANSFORMATIONS FOR MORE RELEVANT, ENGAGING, AND ETHICAL EDUCATION

Creating Eutopian Alternatives Through Education System Transformation

Since schools possess an enormous amount of power in shaping the ideologies and practices of the broader populace, they are institutions which must develop foresight and provide a response to the world's greatest challenges (the poverty, starvation, war, discrimination, and environmental degradation that characterise the contemporary world). The notion that alternative (or superior) futures need to be 'imagined' suggests that many aspects of the past and present have somehow been / are unsatisfactory. Indeed, the point of envisioning, and working to realise, preferable futures (and the subsequent transformation of wider society in order to design strategies to achieve those desirable visions) is to create a world that is instead distinguished by equity, peace, and sustainability.

As institutionalised education is typically offered to the young (that is, people who have not been overly conditioned by limiting ideologies of nationalism and self-interest), there exists the chance to introduce to them notions of how to think and behave in a manner that is ethical in a global context. Thus, in accepting that a widely adopted education system has the power to influence and shape the beliefs and behaviours of massive numbers of people, incorporating Indigenous, Holistic, Multicultural, and Futures knowledges into contemporary schools could result in the emergence of whole societies of ethical citizens, all committed to transforming the world through acts of compassion, tolerance, respect, social justice, and ecological preservation. To provide a forum in which to explore and generate alternative and preferable realities, education systems could also be based on the social reconstruction model. Such a model foregrounds the critique of existing ideologies, discourses, and systems which create and maintain global problems, as well as the reconstruction of both local and international society along more ethical guidelines. By visualising preferred futures, pupils have a platform from which to engage in a critique of the past and present, as well as a goal to work towards in devising strategies to transform and improve the world.

This chapter will explore why alterations of the current Western education model are necessary, and how such transformations can be realised in classrooms around the world. A proposed Transitionary Education Model (for countries still solely utilising nature-damaging and inequity-creating Industrial Era models) is featured in the next chapter, and it can be immediately implemented in learning institutions to ensure that Western approaches to curriculum, pedagogy, and evaluation are now balanced by Indigenous, Holistic, Multicultural, and Futures knowledges and practices.

The Purpose of Futures-Based Education System Transformation

The aim of transforming the dominant education system is to focus contemporary global populations on devising and implementing solutions for those situations which are, at present, most serious and pressing. High priority issues (which trend extrapolations suggest will continue to be of great importance well into the future) include: creating sustainable societies to guarantee intergenerational environmental health; fostering conditions that encourage humanity to embrace peace-promoting ideologies and practices; adopting equity-creating social and economic structures; and working to ensure holistic health for diverse global populations.

By employing a variety of thinking methods (for example, critical, alternative, divergent, lateral, spiritual, moral, compassionate) and consulting traditional Indigenous peoples and cultures for guidance regarding locally beneficial wisdoms, students can work to transform those unethical and corrupt economic, political, legal, and social systems that are currently dominant. This may in turn provide inspiration for politicians and public servants (including education system bureaucrats) to honour their international obligations, and for all of humanity to prioritise healing over indulging in the harm-generating acts of capitalistic greed, the pursuit of power in discriminatory hierarchies, and extensive engagement in excessive consumption and materialism (as well as the environmental degradation and violence and war which such behaviours give rise to).

Since it is the young who are inheriting a future world that is phenomenally uncertain for billions of people (in terms of where they will be able to live safely, sustainably, and healthily), it is essential young people are immediately empowered to find solutions for the global problems which they themselves will soon be facing and managing. Transforming education systems to incorporate Futures knowledges is thus essential if students are to be provided with the opportunities and power to devise and implement long-term solutions to the world's most pressing concerns.

For example, instead of offering only rationalist academic or technical (vocational) courses that aim to perpetuate the social inequities and environmental destruction typical of the Industrial Era, schools may need to devise a curriculum that focuses on social reconstruction through critique and alteration of the status quo. Participation and empowerment are the key characteristics of the social reconstruction model, and students from all cultural backgrounds, possessing a range of talents and skills (not just the ones related to Western forms of literacy and numeracy), should be granted equal status in the construction of futures that feature fairer economic and social systems. To alleviate disengagement from learning, greater attempts could also be made to ignite the passions of students by encouraging them to embrace higher causes, thereby enabling them to make meaningful contributions to the wider community. Giving pupils the freedom to complete self-selected projects that have real-world impact can further help them to realise the desirable futures that they themselves wish to create. In terms of pedagogy, educational practitioners may need to abandon individualistic activities that lead to negative competitive behaviours in favour of constructivist and collaborative approaches which encourage active and cooperative involvement in envisioning, and determining how to manifest, preferred collective futures. Meanwhile, on an organisational level, schools may find that the traditional timetables, facilities, and daily duties of educators have to be altered to accommodate the distinct curriculum, evaluation, and pedagogical policies required for successful implementation of the practices related to the teaching of Futures knowledges.

The Lack of Contemporary Relevance of Dominant Schooling Curricula and Practices

There are a number of Western schooling practices that are still dominant and which must be transformed if institutional forms of education are to have any meaningful relevance in the Twenty-First Century. In evaluating the primary challenges that schools currently face, Professor Geoff Masters notes that Western curricula are still dominated by large bodies of 'factual knowledge' at a time when it is more important for students to apply deep understandings of concepts and principles to real-world problems. He also explores the fact that curricula are often designed for delivery in traditional classroom settings and emphasise passive, reproductive learning and the solution of standard problem types, even though there is a growing need for transformations in how learning takes place and the ability of students to develop innovative solutions to new global issues. Furthermore, he says that school subjects are still taught (and assessed and reported on) in isolation from each other (via traditional disciplines), but societal challenges must actually be dealt with in a cross-disciplinary way. As well, in Western schools students often learn in competition with each other despite the fact that collaboration, teamwork, and good interpersonal and communication skills are increasingly important.

Ways to Transform Curriculum

In the current Western education system, highly prescriptive syllabuses, outcomes, and standards statements consistently work to narrow the curriculum, control student thought, quash imagination, and perpetuate a style of education that generates more social problems than it solves. By implementing a consciousness-raising approach to curriculum, educators can stop simply observing or analysing those elements of the world that can be viewed as dystopian in character, and instead take a proactive stance by suggesting that a preferable state of affairs can be initially visualised, and subsequently worked towards, through deliberate transformative actions taken by students (either as individuals or in small or large groups).

Preferred visions of the future are already being developed on a frequent basis by a large number of International Non-Governmental Organisations (such as Amnesty International and Global Citizen) and various United Nations bodies (via documents like the *Universal Declaration of Human Rights*). Many Futurists have also outlined their personal visions of what would constitute a global society free from widespread suffering (a commitment to non-violence, environmental protection, and social justice all being particularly high on several agendas), however people all throughout the world can (and should) be involved in collectively determining which ethical realities are the best ones to pursue for an harmonious shared existence. Only through direct participation in envisioning these realities can global citizens experience a sense of connection to their preferred futures, and so feel motivated and empowered to take the required steps to achieve them. Many theorists believe that human beings are more hopeful and positive when they are involved in meeting challenges and crises with action – that is, actively being part of the process of social change and transformation.

So, while a multitude of divergent beliefs currently exist with respect to what would characterise an 'ideal' world, it is only through pluralistic debate, underpinned by a commitment to broader ethical concerns, that students from vastly different cultural, economic, and political backgrounds can begin to develop visions of preferable futures which may result in the implementation of effective solutions to global problems. It is therefore essential that young people are allowed to determine those global concerns that are most pressing, and to exert collective control over which preferred futures they should be working to create - the emphasis now being on student action and social transformation rather than mere 'regurgitation' of existing forms of Western knowledge.

As such, whilst educators can provide opportunities for their pupils to be exposed to a range of contemporary issues, it is crucial that the latter are provided with the freedom to establish their own identities, make their own decisions, and engage with causes that are of greatest personal significance. Students can do this by constructing their own contextualised and problem-oriented curriculum that works to benefit the community in ways that they determine are appropriate. Young people need to be allowed to devise their own solutions to the problems that the world presents them with – indeed, as they are the ones inheriting the Earth, they have a right to determine how to transform the status quo, as well as how to create preferable social conditions for humanity.

When schools offer predetermined academic and vocational courses, they essentially prevent the young from freely choosing and shaping the future (including their own destinies and the fate of the entire planet). Self-selected and open-ended projects that ask pupils to make real-world impacts on the larger community (local, national, and / or global) are far more empowering and require students to critique contemporary society and make value judgements about which aspects are worth preserving and which need to be transformed. From this point, pupils can then envision preferable futures, build scenarios, and devise strategies for making their eutopian ideals become reality. In this way the curriculum becomes interesting, relevant, and engaging for students, as they are given the chance to define what is important and thus have a personal connection to their studies. In freely exploring social issues and fighting for higher causes, pupils also develop a greater sense of life purpose and are more likely to be engaged in meaningful activities. Ultimately, unless young people are provided with the opportunity to determine their own curriculum, there will always be the risk that mandated topics of study merely reflect the personal concerns and interests of the adults devising the units - in other words, those with power will continue to define what is supposedly 'essential knowledge', and so construct the world in an extremely narrow way. Hence, the Futures education model gives learning current relevance and a liberating and empowering dimension by providing pupils with the skills of social activism, as well as a chance at real-life influence on society in the solving of contemporary problems and the construction of preferable alternative realities.

In the course of implementing a consciousness-raising approach to curriculum, it is also essential that educators guide pupils to develop such qualities as understanding, empathy, compassion, tolerance, and respect (that is, in order for them to become aware global citizens), as well as the cognitive processes and bodies of knowledge required by them to envision, design, and realise their preferred futures. Educational institutions could, then, make efforts to transform themselves into 'communities of care' in which humanitarian values are foregrounded at all times. While the philosophy of 'care' can be embraced in the classroom environment itself, it should also be extended into the wider community (on a local, national, and international scale) such that students become attached to concerns that are higher than 'the self'. Young people need to be valued and empowered as global changemakers who can make a positive difference in the world. In this way, a sense of meaning, purpose, and personal significance is brought into their lives, and focus for many at-risk pupils is shifted from internal angst to external concern about broader social issues. Such a curriculum should also be action-oriented, as depression can be exacerbated if students are disempowered in the classroom – that is, if they are merely given knowledge about the problems that exist in contemporary society, but not the skills or opportunities to work at resolving them.

Connectedness can, for instance, be achieved through units that focus on interdependence, cooperation, cultural diversity, wellness, and conflict resolution.

Finally, teachers can aim to facilitate philosophical discussion, critical thinking, and ethical debate, as well as act as consultants and guides for students by encouraging them to engage in processes of interpreting, analysing, questioning, critiquing, challenging, decision-making, and transforming in order to redesign those systems, institutions, and aspects of human behaviour which have led, internationally, to problematic social, economic, and environmental situations. Essentially, underlying Western belief systems and approaches to knowledge must be properly understood and problematised in order for real cultural innovation and recovery to occur. Thus, under a Futures model, students need to connect and apply their learning to everyday experiences, and real-world projects should have an ethical dimension and demand a level of social activism from the participants. Ultimately, offering a curriculum that focuses on pupils developing higher causes, actively caring for the wider community, and devising solutions for real-world problems is a Futures-based approach that can be adopted by educational institutions.

Ways to Transform Methods of Evaluation and Pedagogy

Innovators working in educational contexts also need to devise appropriate evaluation policies and methods to complement Futures-based curriculum transformations. For instance, rather than using standardised tests and abstract assignment tasks that draw on the preferred genres and values of a single state's / nation's dominant cultural group, pupils could be provided with the opportunity to conceptualise and launch international projects that address the needs of the pluralistic global community. As well, rather than utilising activities and assessment items that are abstract in nature and fail to relate to real-world contexts, schools could use open-ended tasks in which students are evaluated (rather than graded and ranked) on their ability to explore and devise effective solutions to global problems. Learning institutions could further develop a policy for the educators, members of the wider community, and the students themselves (including their peers) to jointly evaluate how effective the projects prove to be in offering solutions to real-world problems in the global context. Feedback could take the form of suggestions for how to improve various aspects of the projects, or guidance on the next steps to be taken in realising the construction of preferable futures. Thus, rather than reducing student performance to a series of numbers or letters (through grades and ranks) or checking off prescriptive outcomes in discrete key learning areas, pupils could be provided with more meaningful advice on the actions they need to take in order to embrace humanitarian values and achieve ethical ends.

As well, rather relying on the standard 'broadcast learning' pedagogical model (where the teacher stands at the front of the room and tries to inculcate the passive students with their 'knowledge'), Futures-oriented education demands that a more constructivist approach be utilised. In this way, teachers become facilitators of learning, while the pupils are empowered to use them - as well as many other sources - for drawing on in the construction of their visions and strategies for achieving preferred futures. Taking on a facilitative role means that the pedagogical expertise of educators actually becomes more sophisticated than in traditional classrooms, where simple 'chalk and talk' or textbook and worksheet activities are dominant. Indeed, to successfully guide constructivist-style learning, educators need to be adept at: running meaningful class discussions where appropriate questions are posed to encourage deeper and ethical consideration of complex issues; monitoring small group work and providing effective motivation to keep the learners engaged; providing practical activities which allow the pupils to develop their critical thinking skills; and producing deconstructed models and scaffolds (as a form of overt instruction) to assist the students in producing high quality visions, projects, and global solutions. Teachers should also ensure that they are familiar with the Productive Pedagogies and therefore draw on students' background knowledge to assist the latter with the integration of new knowledges, as well as connect all learning materials to the real world and utilise problem-based approaches to promote active pupil engagement in classroom activities. In addition, teachers need to ensure that a range of student learning styles are catered for to maintain maximum engagement – for instance, some adolescents find too many Western curriculum and assessment activities to be excessively abstract in nature; some Indigenous children find Western learning approaches to be exclusively focused on written literacy (rather than oral and kinaesthetic tasks); and many pupils have a preference for visual over auditory learning styles (and thus disengage whenever a teacher stands at the front of the classroom and talks for long periods of time). As Futures approaches emphasise participation and transformative action in the development of alternative realities, the inevitable implication for Western educational contexts is that a constructivist pedagogical approach be adopted in order to empower young people, thereby giving them the right to construct their own contextualised and problem-oriented curriculum.

Educational institutions that seek to embrace Futures philosophies also need to preference collaborative learning practices. The skills involved in making teamwork a successful endeavour (such as how to negotiate, compromise, and engage in effective conflict resolution) may need to be demonstrated to students on a periodic basis in order for collective futures to be envisioned cooperatively. The increasingly multicultural nature of many contemporary classrooms; the new opportunities for links to other communities and students around the world; the growing development of an appreciation for multi-age classes; and the productive connections being formed with members of each school's wider community, all suggest that it is possible for more pluralistic and global visions to be developed. For students to listen to a range of voices; come to appreciate multiple points of view; and grow to respect diverse peoples, they must be offered the chance to frequently alter, and learn how to interact and cope with, all kinds of collaborative groupings. Cooperative learning can also provide pupils with the opportunity to draw on (and have peer modelling of) a range of talents and abilities which, when combined, will result in the production of better-quality projects and more effective solutions to world troubles. As they move from group to group, students may find that they are being exposed to, or are being forced to develop, different talents and skills with each transition. For a balanced approach and to foster qualities of independence, there is still a place for individual reflection and work (to focus specifically, for instance, on personal skill areas that need to be enhanced). Independent learning should not, however, be characterised by competition or an institutional desire to class some students as intellectually 'superior' and others as possessing 'deficits'. Indeed, educational institutions need to seriously reflect on how their practices are responsible for the occurrence of disengagement, and all educators need to strongly resist theories of 'student deficit' – whole sections of communities cannot be 'blamed' if they refuse to respond to the Western style of education that is being universally imposed on them by inflexible bureaucratic organisations. (Such so-called 'deficits' are, in fact, quite often the opposite – for example, Aboriginal students in Australia frequently possess detailed knowledge of an Indigenous language and unique cultural practices, however in the context of a curriculum and educational setting dominated by the English language and Western ideologies, administrators, and teachers, they are regularly constructed as being intellectually 'inferior'.) Thus, for contemporary students to envision and create futures that are free from intolerance of difference and violence, educational sites must promote (global) collaborative learning and not allow only homogenised teaching voices and visions to be dominant.

A Journey of Hope, Action, and Transformation

Ultimately, contemporary educators may have to admit that they have been part of a culture and generation that has perpetuated war, large-scale environmental degradation, and massive social injustice, while young people, given the time, resources, and freedom of thought, might have effective problem-solving strategies that they wish to implement in the real world. For educators, then, the message is clear – a spirit of experimentation and reform must be capitalised on if genuine solutions are to be found for student disengagement from learning, and if schools are to realise the influence they have in shaping the ideologies and behaviours of massive numbers of people, and so help in achieving world peace, environmental sustainability, and the universal equality of all human beings. Education institutions must also transform themselves into centres where collaborative learning and evaluation of student work that promotes improvement (rather than competition) are foregrounded. To put the ideals into practice, those invested with the most significant decision-making powers in the education system must firstly embrace the vision of a world where all people work to create harmony, and then find practical ways to distribute funds so as to establish schools with ethical agendas. After this, a more realistic journey of hope, action, and transformation can begin – a journey that may, in the future, result in planet Earth and its inhabitants enjoying a collectively preferred reality.

CHAPTER 2
A TRANSITIONARY EDUCATION MODEL THAT AIMS TO GENERATE A PREFERABLE FUTURE FOR HUMANITY AND THE ENVIRONMENT

MONDAY – FRIDAY	PROPOSED CURRICULUM, PEDAGOGY, AND EVALUATION PROGRAMME THAT INCORPORATES FUTURES-BASED EDUCATIONAL THEORY AND CATERS TO WESTERN, INDIGENOUS, HOLISTIC, AND MULTICULTURAL KNOWLEDGES
SESSION 1 9:00-9:30 AM	**Western Education Model** Critical, Alternative, Divergent, and Lateral Thinking; Theory and Ideology Studies; Logic, Philosophy, and Ethics; and Metacognitive Learning Activities
9:30-10:10 10:10-10:50 AM	**Literacy Activities** **Numeracy Activities** **Curriculum** Traditional Western Key Learning Areas (in line with any current National Curriculum) can be delivered through the Literacy and Numeracy Activities sessions on a term-by-term rotational basis. For instance, the Literacy Activities session may involve one lesson per week of operational literacy tasks (dedicated to skills-based spelling, punctuation, grammar, and vocabulary exercises) and one lesson per week of independent reading, but the other three lessons could be dedicated to guided reading, genre modelling / scaffolding, and writing tasks through the traditional Western subjects of English, Studies of Society and the Environment (SOSE), The Arts, and Languages Other Than English (LOTE). Similarly, the Numeracy Activities session may involve one skills lesson per week, but the other lessons could be delivered through traditional Western subjects – rotated on a term-by-term basis – like Maths, Science, Technology, and Physical Education.

	Pedagogy It would be appropriate to preference utilisation of the Productive Pedagogies* in these sessions. Early and regular intervention (such as in the form of individualised and specialised tuition) may also be necessary for English as a Second Language, Special Needs, and other identified students. **Evaluation** It would be appropriate to use assessment items favoured by any current National Curriculum under this model.
SESSION 2 **11:10-11:40 AM**	**Holistic and Futures Education Models** **Non-Competitive Health and Well-Being Activities** (for example, Yoga; Qigong; Feldenkrais; Tai Chi; Meditation; World Dance; Nutritional Food Preparation; Spiritual, Emotional, and Mental Health and Well-Being Tasks; and so on).
11:40 AM – 12:20 PM	**Futures-Based Holistic Learning and Knowledges Lecture** **Curriculum** Holistic educators deliver large-group lectures on topics relevant to four central Futures Themes: Global Peace and Harmony; Sustainability and Environmental Stewardship; Equity and Social Justice in Multicultural Societies; and Body, Mind, and Soul Matters. Western-trained teachers may find that material they once delivered in other subjects can be easily modified to fit into these Themes. For instance, former Geography and Science teachers may already have many resources related to notions of climate change (Sustainability and Environmental Stewardship), while former History teachers may have existing materials about Gandhi and peaceful ways to achieve racial equality (for Global Peace and Harmony). All holistic educators should, however, expand their bodies of knowledge so as to also deliver lectures in more typical Ecological and New Age fields. Former Home Economics teachers could, for instance, prepare lectures on the healing properties of organic and native foods (Body, Mind,

	and Soul Matters), while former Art teachers could hold lectures on the role of intuition and dream analysis in the artistic process (as has been favoured by Western, Eastern, and Indigenous artists) as a way to explore issues related to Equity and Social Justice in Multicultural Societies.
12:20-1:00 PM	**Self-Directed Shaping the Future Project Work** **<u>Futures Project Work</u>** Students work in different term-long, inter-age configurations (for example, as individuals, in pairs, or small or large groups) on their own, personally-determined, 'Shaping a Better Future' projects. The term-long projects should revolve around the four central Futures Themes stated above, and are to be delivered / published / released / performed / enacted in the real world. The projects should be interdisciplinary, multicultural (local), or international in flavour, and they may be delivered in any mode (oral, written, or visual) and utilising any number of genres (for example, documentary, academic journal article, musical CD, research assignment, live play, website, dance performance, pamphlet, blog, analytical essay, poster, storyboard, newspaper column, and so on). The projects are not to be graded. Students will, however, be required to engage in oral and written self-evaluation (including of the short- and long-term real-world impact of their efforts). The holistic educators and students' peers, family, and community members will also be requested to provide progressive oral, then a final written, evaluation regarding the overall quality of the work (as well as where improvements could be made in subsequent submissions). Students should not repeat aspects of each term's project (the theme, focus, or genres favoured) in the course of a year. Files containing details and elements of the four projects each student works on annually should be maintained.

	Pedagogy Holistic educators are to act as consultants, providing knowledge, advice, research materials, critical feedback, and assistance when requested by students (who make set consultation bookings when they feel they need additional guidance). Students can also utilise their own resources for the completion of all project work.
SESSION 3 **1:30-3:00 PM**	**Indigenous Education Model** **Traditional Living Activities With Indigenous Community Members** (for example, Languages; Art; Music; Dance; Rituals and Ceremonies; Law; Gathering and Hunting; Caring for Country; Storytelling; Dreaming; and so on). **Curriculum** As above, or, where delivery of such learning is not physically possible, students are to complete term-long courses in **Indigenous Studies** (for example, Comparative Study of Global Indigenous Cultures; Black Politics; World History; Anthropology; Appreciation and Analysis of Contemporary and Traditional Indigenous Artistic and Cultural Pursuits: Film, Literature, Music, Theatre, Art, Television, Dance; and so on), which may be delivered by non-Indigenous educators. **Pedagogy** Traditional Indigenous methods of teaching / learning (for example, a focus on non-competitive forms of discussion / storytelling; observation and imitation in artistic pursuits; and so on) are to be favoured. **Oral Evaluation** Educators orally evaluate whether students have developed deep knowledge and understanding - and a respectful appreciation - of traditional and contemporary Indigenous cultures.

*THE PRODUCTIVE PEDAGOGIES

Intellectual Quality
- Higher Order Thinking
- Deep Knowledge
- Deep Understanding
- Substantive Conversation
- Knowledge as Problematic
- Metalanguage

Relevance
- Knowledge Integration
- Background Knowledge
- Connectedness to the World
- Problem Based Curriculum

Supportive Classroom Environment
- Student Control
- Social Support
- Engagement
- Explicit Criteria
- Self-Regulation

Recognition of Difference
- Cultural Knowledges
- Inclusivity
- Narrative
- Group Identity
- Citizenship

[The Queensland School Reform Longitudinal Study Research Team (2001) *Theoretical Rationale for the Development of Productive Pedagogies: A Literature Review.* St Lucia (Brisbane): The University of Queensland, Graduate School of Education.]

'Shaping a Better Future' Project Ideas for the Sustainability and Environmental Stewardship Theme

1. Students could develop a range of practical and immediate strategies for dismantling industrial and technology-dependent societies in order to ensure intergenerational environmental health and the survival of a large number of animal species and humanity itself. While many politicians advocate 'personal lifestyle choices' which keep capitalism intact, humanity

cannot actually consume its way out of environmental collapse (since consumption itself is the problem). Industrialism and the imperatives of growth and production will no doubt need to be abandoned. The systems that are destroying the planet - industrial agriculture; extractive industries like mining, fishing, and logging; and the fossil fuel infrastructure – will also need to be replaced with sustainable local ecosystems.

2. Students could devise a number of ways for humanity to live without reliance on environmentally destructive forms of energy. The vast majority of water and energy use is by the world's commercial, industrial, corporate, agribusiness, government, and military bodies, and even green, renewable, or 'clean' technologies require high-polluting infrastructures at every point in the production process (for example, the manufacture of wind turbines produces radioactive and carcinogenic waste). Indeed, a world run by solar, wind, hydro, geothermal, or biofuels power would inevitably feature global industrial mining, manufacturing and transportation infrastructures, along with all the natural resource exploitation they involve. Students could therefore work out how damage-free forms of energy can be generated (such as via mind power) and utilised, or how humanity can most harmoniously return to pre-industrial lifestyles in which unsustainable forms of energy are simply not required.

3. Students could compare the environmentally sustainable survival methods (including underpinning ideologies and practices) of various Indigenous peoples with the more ecologically damaging means of survival favoured by Westerners. For instance, in an 1800s speech, Suquamish and Duwamish (Native American) Chief Seattle questions the extremely environmentally destructive actions of Westerners – their over-population of the land; heavy technology dependency; and extensive removal of flora and habitat destruction of fauna (including wholesale slaughtering of the buffalo). By contrast, Indigenous peoples imbue the land with spiritual value and develop a familial relationship between themselves and all of nature. [See Appendix A for an extended excerpt from Chief Seattle's speech.] Students could thus look to vastly wiser and more caring and compassionate traditional-living Indigenous communities to solve the problems of Western society and the massive damage that it has caused for the environment, all wildlife species, and the people of the planet as a whole. Revitalising Indigenous wisdom is, therefore, a sensible

long-term solution, as the traditional custodians were able to live sustainably and healthily for thousands of years prior to Western interference. By using Indigenous knowledges from all across the world as inspiration, students could determine how to rebuild just and sustainable communities where ideologies of responsibility and sacrifice are more important than entitlement and greed.

'Shaping a Better Future' Project Ideas for the Global Peace and Harmony Theme

One of the main consequences of the West's long-term commitment to violence and war in the assertion of its economic, political, and cultural power, is that an extremely large number of poor and disadvantaged peoples are now at-risk or displaced - many suffering in, or fleeing, lands where complex conflicts have emerged because of colonial and post-colonial interferences. The sheer number of humans currently living in insecure and transient conditions means that there is a high-priority need to provide safe accommodation and adequate care for all refugees, asylum seekers, and peoples living in war zones, as well as slaves, political prisoners, and those who are homeless or survivors of physical abuse on domestic fronts. In line with the Global Peace and Harmony Futures Theme, then, students could use compassionate, alternative, and ethical forms of thinking to develop projects that prioritise solutions for those seeking temporary or permanent refuge. It is also essential that pupils find ways for humanity to abandon the ideologies and practices that generate highly violent relations between peoples throughout the world in the first place. Some ideas to inspire students in their development of 'Shaping a Better Future' Projects are listed below.

1. Students could develop compassionate and viable solutions for the safe movement of the growing numbers of at-risk and displaced persons currently traversing the planet. For instance, they could explore the notion that all the world's nations contribute to the funding of a body led by the United Nations (UN) that actively goes into each country and determines how many people are seeking asylum or refuge and the best methods for providing them with safe passage out. Ultimately, in line with fundamental human rights protections, there must be an immediate end to the current situation of leaving vulnerable peoples in dangerous situations without external assistance. In other words, at-risk and displaced individuals

should not be left with no other option but to engage in unlawful actions like paying 'people smugglers' or taking to the seas (risking drowning, thirst, and starvation) or jungle tracks (risking capture, exploitation in labour camps, and murder) simply in the hope that they will achieve long-term safety and survival.

2. Students could use alternative and ethical thinking to find solutions for the immediate, short- and long-term accommodation and care of refugees and asylum seekers after they have been provided with safe passage (that is, in ways other than human rights-breaching forms of 'indefinite detention'). For instance, using Hong Kong and Singapore as inspiration (that is, small land masses that house millions of people), the UN could request that each country donate its uninhabited islands for formation of a new 'multicultural global nation' to house all the world's displaced persons (called, perhaps, The Refugee Islands), with a UN-elected Council providing interim administration. The billions that many governments currently spend on 'border protection' could then be redirected to these islands (for the building of shelters, the implementation of water systems, the importation of food, and so on) until the resident populations are able to establish their own functioning economies and political structures.

3. Students could devise strategies for the elimination of weapons of violence and war on all continents of the planet. For instance, pupils could lobby politicians to propose bills that ban the importation and sale of guns and bullets in a given country, or they could develop a plan for the dismantling of military infrastructure and operations in all nations.

'Shaping a Better Future' Project Ideas for the Equity and Social Justice in Multicultural Societies Theme

In attempts to eliminate the ideologies, practices, and behaviours that generate inequity and social injustice in contemporary societies (and thereby transform globally dominant and harmful political, economic, legal, and social systems), many ideas for 'Shaping a Better Future' Projects can be suggested to pupils of all ages.

1. Students could devise a series of campaigns to challenge the dominant beliefs and systems which are particularly problematic in terms of creating social inequities. In many countries, for instance, empowerment or disempowerment occurs as a result of the operation of highly defined social, economic, legal, and political

hierarchies which can be questioned and dismantled. Students could also challenge and transform those practices which have led to excessive amounts of wealth, land, and material possessions being concentrated into the hands of a few, while millions face the realities of malnutrition and survival-threatening poverty each day. By working with organisations like Global Citizen, World Vision, Oxfam, or Oz Harvest, students can come to understand the philosophies of redistribution and equitable distribution, then develop political and economic policies which reflect more ethical and fairer ways of sharing the world's resources.

2. Students could go on bush camps with traditional Australian Aboriginal community members to learn how the latter and their ancestors favour/ed forms of survival that actively work against ideologies of land ownership, materialism, and monetary-based operations (as they have done for over 70,000 years). Students could also create stories and songlines to show how the concept of 'shame' is used (for example, in parables or gentle forms of teasing) to restore equality and justice when individuals fail to share, cooperate, and maintain equitable status with others. By participating in gathering, hunting, and other survival-related practices, pupils can further come to appreciate the fact that men and women in traditional Australian Aboriginal societies are valued equally for their social roles and functions. As well, young people can come to understand notions of political equity under a participatory democracy model, as Aboriginal Elders (regardless of gender) are respected and appreciated for their wisdom, but they are not elected leaders and all decisions are made through evolving forms of consensus within a kinship clan. Finally, students could develop step-by-step programmes aimed at returning all land to local Indigenous populations (and subsequently revitalising traditional cultural practices), such that there is a restoration of justice and equity in colonised areas.

3. Students could work towards guaranteeing greater forms of justice and more equitable resource distribution by ensuring that the planet is not over-populated, and that proper environmental health can be maintained with fewer people to feed, accommodate, and care for. Given that it took millions of years (until the 1800s) for the world's human population to reach 1 billion, and it will have taken less than another 250 years to grow by more than 8 billion (to reach a projected 9 to 10 billion in

2050), an immediate reduction in world population (and especially of the highest-consuming, heaviest resource-using, and biggest-polluting peoples) should be a major priority for humanitarian reasons. Pupils could thus devise a range of strategies for rapidly decreasing human populations, from paying males to have (reversible) vasectomies to providing free contraception to all post-pubescent women.

'Shaping a Better Future' Project Ideas for the Body, Mind, and Soul Matters Theme

1. Students could engage in a comparative investigation of the spiritually-based physical activities of a range of Eastern cultures. After learning about such disciplines as Yoga and Qigong, pupils could then devise ways to share their understanding of the relevant philosophies and practices with the wider community in order to promote good physical health, strength, and fitness (and so counter rising obesity rates).

2. Students could apply different models of psychological analysis to their own lives, thought processes, and behaviours – for instance, the psychodynamic approaches of Freud and Jung, or the various methods favoured by behaviourist, humanist, personal growth, and cognitive models. Such insights could then be used by pupils to enhance their own writing in a range of genres.

3. Students could compile a list of the philosophical similarities between various spiritual beliefs across the world by interviewing key figures or reading relevant texts from diverse faiths. Students could then engage in acts of mindfulness through meditation and contemplate how to incorporate shared ethical and spiritual understandings into the fabric of their everyday lives.

4. Students could attend Holistic Living Expos and participate in workshops on topics like intuition, metaphysical healing, and creative visualisation.

Futures-Based 'Create A Better World' Community Planning Ideas

Many of the ideas in this section have been discussed in local community planning sessions, with several participants suggesting a range of the recommended actions. The publisher can be contacted for additional information regarding the culturally and age diverse workshop participants, including what specific recommendations they made. Educators may like to run their own 'Create a Better World' Community Planning Events in order to focus student attention on important global issues and what specific actions they can take to bring about positive change.

Issues of Greatest Community Concern:

Existential Threats
1. Environment-Related Threats to Survival
- Climate Change
- Species Extinction (Bees)
- Pandemics resulting from explosion of rats and bats due to extinction of large animals
2. Nuclear Annihilation
3. Annihilation by Artificial Intelligence (AI)

Moral Issues
4. Equity Issues
5. Social Justice Issues
6. Environmental Stewardship Issues
7. Peace and Harmony Issues

Human Well-Being Matters
8. Physical Health
9. Mental & Emotional Well-Being
10. Spiritual Awareness and Connectedness

Environment-Related Recommended Actions:

Personal Level: Dramatically reduce personal levels of consumption (materialism). Take personal responsibility for every environment-polluting action, then discontinue it (for example, by not flying) or offset it (for example., by planting native trees).

Local Level: Take immediate and extensive action to implement strategies that result in a massive reduction of carbon emissions. Identify the lowest polluting areas in the world and make adoption of parallel modes of operation the highest priority.

State Level: Completely transform educational curricula to ensure that humanity is being taught how to minimise pollution and live sustainably. Replace 'human capital' models of education with traditional Indigenous and holistic models.

National Level: Design a national curricula focused on environmental stewardship. Introduce legislation to compel all members of society to measure their 'carbon footprint', then to be accountable for significantly reducing or offsetting their impact on the environment.

Global Level: Improve mechanisms for holding the highest-polluting countries to account. Design global education curricula around sustainability and ideologies that do not create existential threats for humanity, then pass the approaches on to educators in the most relevant countries.

Recommended Actions Regarding Various Moral Issues:
Personal Level: Show personal respect to all peoples, creatures, and environments. Prioritise understanding, tolerance, compassion, care, and love in all interactions.
Local Level: Engage human rights lawyers to ensure that bureaucrats adhere to all social justice policies (pertaining to the identities of diverse populations).
State Level: Make education about contribution, connectedness, and collaboration rather than individualism and competition ('rankings').
National Level: Use a suite of economic legislative reforms to create a more equitable society (for example, eliminate gender pay gaps, trial Universal Income, etc.).
Global Level: Set up a 'United Nations Help Centre' in every major city in the world and allow individuals to access legal assistance for human rights abuses.

Recommended Actions Regarding Human Well-Being Matters:
Personal Level: Take personal responsibility for eating a nutritious diet and transmuting difficult life events into positive opportunities for growth.
Local Level: Establish a Local Well-Being Centre in all areas so that individuals can access activities / referrals to enhance their personal health and happiness.
State Level: Adopt holistic models of education that emphasise healthy eating; spiritual forms of exercise; positive thinking; and harmonious human relations.
National Level: Use legislative measures to make profiting companies financially responsible for causing harm (for example, from junk food, social media abuse, and so on).
Global Level: Establish 'United Nations Global Learning Centres' in every city in the world and make personal well-being support and resources free for all.

Ways to Implement Futures Studies

In *Futures: Tools and Techniques,* Richard Slaughter outlines a range of ways that various themes and concepts can be explored in a Futures-based curriculum. Some of the major approaches he suggests for use are detailed below.

- Cultural Innovation and Social Invention: There is no predetermined future and at any point humanity can innovate to invent its own preferred future. All students can respond constructively to solve the greatest problems of the contemporary era.
- Exploring Alternatives: The field of possible scenarios, events, or lines of development. An exploration of alternatives by students gives rise to choices - depending on values, priorities, and commitments, these choices lead to certain decisions and actions. Choosing from alternatives is about pupils working towards particular desirable destinations.
- Envisioning Preferable Futures: All students can construct images of preferred futures and develop strategies to enable the creation of those futures. Images of the future are provisional, negotiable, and a product of individual or collective will and design – they represent potentials and opportunities for engagement, choice, and action. Invented images let go of the problematic past and open up new possibilities for change.
- Building Scenarios: Scenarios can be developed by students to portray a desired future in order to help create it. When examining scenarios, major ideas, governing assumptions, and value judgements can be identified, while internal coherence can also be assessed. Contrasting scenarios (such as of a collapsing society versus a transforming society) can be constructed by pupils such that vastly different trends can be modelled.
- Critiquing: This approach studies cultural editing (the processes by which cultures choose to construe the world one way and not another) and considers different ways of knowing, values, and epistemologies (which expands the range of possible futures).
- Applied Foresight: Humanity's ability to foresee future problems and make adaptations in advance means that wise choices can be consciously made and the most beneficial alternatives can be consciously selected by students - this is clearly preferable to constant crisis management.

- Empowerment Principle: The notion that resolutions to major fears about the future reside in developing high quality responses to them. In other words, students can channel the energy of anxiety into motivation and devising strategies and social innovations that address the world's most serious problems.
- Reconceptualising: Reconceptualisations can come in the form of new ideas, meanings, proposals, suggestions, and innovations. They can involve students discarding, revising, and renegotiating old worldview assumptions, with higher human motives being used to reshape social systems.
- Creativity: Creative images of preferred futures take humanity beyond the known and the given. Imaginative approaches can help bring pupils freedom from the limitations of the present, thereby opening up new ideas, options, and aspirations. Shifts in perspective can further enhance creativity.

Slaughter also emphasises the value of students developing Futures Webs and Timelines and, in their construction, utilising such skills as are involved in:
- Backcasting;
- Forecasting;
- Scanning;
- Brainstorming;
- Long-Term Thinking;
- Intuiting;
- Researching;
- Interpreting;
- Analysing;
- Evaluating;
- Extrapolating;
- Decision-Making;
- Synthesising;
- Goal-Setting;
- Arguing; and
- Modelling

CHAPTER 3
INDIGENOUS EDUCATION MODEL

Australian Aboriginal Knowledges of Spiritual and Practical Benefit to Contemporary Peoples

Prior to Western invasion, colonisation, imperialism, assimilation, and cultural genocide, Aboriginal peoples residing in the land currently known as 'Australia' managed, for over 70,000 years, to live sustainably and in harmony with the environment; promote high levels of social equity and peace; ensure community-wide care for children in physically healthy and emotionally supportive ways; and maintain a true (consensually-based) form of democracy that was participatory (rather than 'representative') in nature. As such, humanity can look to vastly wiser traditional-living Indigenous peoples for solutions to Western society's deepest contemporary crises, as well as the massive damage that those of Western origin have caused for the environment and the people of the planet as a whole. While Western society often adopts a superior attitude and trivialises Indigenous cultures, knowledges, and wisdoms, it repeatedly fails to recognise that it has imposed life-threatening forms of consumerism on the world. If Westerners were to move beyond their own ignorance, they would be able to learn from traditional forms of connection between people, spirit, and the earth, and thereby see themselves as caretakers of the land rather than its conquerors.

The Benefits of an Indigenous Education Model

One increasingly appealing eutopian alternative to the highly environmentally and socially damaging globalisation of Western beliefs, systems, and institutions is that of the reinvigoration of traditional and local Indigenous ideologies and practices. In particular, the traditional Aboriginal cultures of the land mass now known as Australia offer some extremely effective challenges to dominant Western belief systems by foregrounding notions of ecological sustainability, minimal materialism under non-monetary systems, and social equality through sharing and cooperation. An educational focus on a variety of Indigenous discourses can encourage deeper critiques of capitalist-inspired competition, individualism, and hierarchically and monetary-based inequalities, as well as industrial-style exploitation of natural resources in the name of profit (greed) and materialism. From dominant culture critiques, humanity can then move more readily to building, and realising, scenarios in which many of the eutopia-creating ideologies and practices of traditional Indigenous cultures are dominant.

While schools could certainly facilitate such explorations of eutopian alternatives, their current role as a perpetuator of the status quo (rather than a transformative agent) may be so entrenched that, ultimately, it could prove most fruitful to follow the lead of many Aboriginal kinship clans in Australia and completely abandon institutions of formal education in favour of more holistic styles of learning in the natural environment. Indeed, it is highly problematic to force all children to be part of a system of schooling which occurs in buildings and relies on those same styles of (Western) literacy, numeracy, and science to resolve the very problems that they have given rise to (on a global scale) in the first place. Instead, humanity could most easily create a eutopian future by actually living in the natural world and directly learning the Indigenous ideologies and practices that stress environmental sustainability, responsibility to community, and high degrees of social equality. Ultimately, it may be that schools can best respond to contemporary challenges by restoring the rights of traditional Indigenous communities to provide forms of education which will lead to more eutopian realities for both the natural environment and humanity as a whole.

Australian Aboriginal Ideologies Regarding Natural Environments

The reinvigoration of Indigenous attitudes to the natural environment is one vision of a preferred future that is undoubtedly gaining greater credence. The belief systems of various kinship clans from Aboriginal Australia are particularly valuable for those whose goal it is to build scenarios which feature humans living in harmony with the land and its ecosystems. A dominant Aboriginal ideology is that human beings have a deep spiritual relationship with all animate and inanimate elements of the environment (from wombats and trees to rocks and mountains), and they must therefore honour this bond by observing important responsibilities they have to the natural world. For traditional-living Aboriginal Australians, understanding that the land itself has rights, and caring for the Earth

Mother and its citizens (flora, fauna, and other natural elements and landscapes), means that the people themselves will be cared for in return. Such a philosophy promotes respectful practices, whereby minimal destructive impact is exerted on the land and resources are used moderately because of an overriding belief in replenishment rather than exhaustion. There are a wide range of conservation methods that Aboriginal peoples employ in both their hunting and gathering practices – including only harvesting immature male animals (not reproductive females); ensuring that no unnecessary killing or wastage of food occurs by culling a very small number of animals from each group; engaging in seasonal mobility to allow the resources in each area a chance to replenish; and letting fallen fruit stay on the ground to grow for future seasons. Furthermore, the ability to live without monetary systems and to operate with a limited number of material goods exemplifies how Aboriginal peoples avoid the resource depletion that has accompanied the greed for wealth and products in industrial societies. Prior to British invasion, Australian Aboriginal peoples operated non-money-based economies for tens of thousands of years in a way that resulted in significantly low carbon emissions. Hence, the Aboriginal worldview, in which humans are seen to be an inseparable part of nature (and so not able to dominate it), can provide the basis for constructing an alternative (and perhaps eutopian) future, in which mass destruction of various regional environments does not occur.

As well, when considering how to ensure adequate food to guarantee the nutritional health of global populations, it is interesting to note that Aboriginal peoples successfully managed the Australian continent in a highly sustainable way for over 70,000 years as a result of the maintenance of low and steady populations. Anthropological evidence indicates that despite a rate of infant death slightly higher than that of contemporary Western society, surviving Australian Aborigines actually lived very long and much healthier lives than today's Caucasian population (primarily due to consumption of an extremely nutritional diet, engagement in regular exercise, low levels of stress, and the complete absence of most forms of illness and disease). In spite of good health and thus long lives, Indigenous peoples did not, however, come to overpopulate Australia because they carefully practised a variety of birth control methods (anthropologists have indicated that eating yams and / or having knowledge of fertility in line with women's monthly cycles may have been utilised for contraceptive purposes). By deliberately choosing to only have one or two children per woman, and by living semi-nomadically and never exhausting local resources, long-term environmental sustainability and relative peace between neighbouring (and maritally interconnected) clans was thus possible. Some estimates put the pre-British invasion population of Australia at between one and two million – a figure that did not put undue stress on underground water supplies, native animal habitats, or soil health (in addition to the fact that Indigenous peoples were not living heavy resource-using and highly energy-dependent materialistic lifestyles). As such, Australian Aborigines, through maintenance of low, steady, and environmentally sustainable populations, as well as peace-promoting belief systems, were able to live in a physically healthy way for tens of thousands of years.

Australian Aboriginal Educational Approaches in Relation to Natural Environments

Since Western-style schools play a key role in perpetuating the civilisation that is responsible for so much environmental harm, their main challenge is to abandon those processes which maintain the status quo. For over 70,000 years the Aboriginal peoples of Australia have employed a form of education which ensures that their civilisation does not generate ecological destruction on a global scale. This form of education is holistic in nature and, most importantly, occurs in the natural environment, where real spiritual bonds with the land and its creatures can be formed. Aboriginal peoples regard themselves as being *of* the land and sea (fitting into it and being shaped by it), thus their teachings and stories come from the Earth itself (in other words, the Earth and all its natural features are the centre of their wisdom). Furthermore, the use of material resources is minimised as learning occurs primarily through oral traditions (storytelling), as well as observation and imitation of real-life activities in the natural world, hence 'school' buildings (including desks and chairs), books, paper, pens, and elaborate forms of technology (such as computers, televisions, and laboratory equipment) are not necessary. One result of this kind of education is that Aboriginal children are able to demonstrate a growing respect for, and responsibility to, nature – such outcomes are far more qualitative and ethically-based than the quantifiable abilities to 'read', 'write', 'measure', and 'multiply' that are emphasised in the early years of Western-style schooling. Fundamental to learning traditional and ancient ways of survival is Aboriginal peoples' recognition of a spiritual affiliation with nature. Therefore, for schools to meet the challenge of altering the dominant civilisation's lack of respect for the environment, their best response may be to relinquish control of uniformly educating the masses and, instead, restore the powers of various Indigenous communities to pass on their wisdom via nature-based learning.

Australian Aboriginal Ideologies Regarding Equity and Peace

By problematising the unequal distribution of wealth and power (including military, and hence warring, capacity) in contemporary times, educators can also claim a legitimate reason for having students envision preferred futures, build scenarios around these preferences, and devise the means to realise eutopian alternatives. One vision of a desirable future that is growing in prominence is the adoption of traditional Indigenous philosophies and customs that emphasise the importance of community and cooperation. In particular, the equitable relations that are fundamental to the operation of many kinship clans in Aboriginal Australia provide a valuable base for the construction of fairer future scenarios. For example, much inspiration can be derived from the form of participatory democracy that is favoured in decision-making processes within Aboriginal societies. Under this system, hierarchically-based relations are minimised as different members of each clan are seen to hold specialised knowledge (this includes both men and women) and thus, in combination with the smallness of their populations, this means that all community participants can contribute to the making of key political decisions. Aboriginal kinship clans have no official 'leaders', and while the wisdom of the Elders is commonly respected and consulted, the decisions of the larger group are achieved by the progressive evolution of consensus (to support the operation of this system, hostility is explicitly displayed towards people who appear to be motivated by status or power). Additionally, the gathering and hunting lifestyle engaged in by Aboriginal peoples ensures that no individual can acquire significant amounts of land, money, or material goods.

Equity between clan members is further promoted by the dominance of ideologies and practices which foreground cooperation and sharing. In fact, specific punishments exist if any person tries to increase their status (for example, by being a consistently better hunter than others), or if they fail to evenly distribute their gathered foods with the entire group. For traditionally-oriented Australian Aboriginal peoples, unity and sharing are prioritised over division and hoarding. Furthermore, due to their seasonal movements to areas of abundance, deprivation or poverty for a certain percentage of peoples is never an ongoing reality – careful methods of birth control also ensure that no large populations are left suffering in landscapes with natural resources that cannot sufficiently support their survival. Finally, the establishment of alliances and extended kinship relations (via intermarriage) with neighbouring clans means that the potential for unequal and violent / war-based relations across groups (via military dominance or exploitative imperialistic activity) is greatly minimised. Peaceful inter-clan relations are further supported by the fact that in Aboriginal cosmology, everything and everybody, all space and all time, is intertwined and interdependent - all are kin. Clearly then, humanity can work to construct a more eutopian alternative future by embracing those traditional Indigenous ideologies and practices which result in legitimate forms of equality and long-term peace between all peoples.

Australian Aboriginal Educational Approaches Promoting Peace and Equity

If the education system can be held largely responsible for the way a civilisation functions, then a significant challenge that Western-style schools face is to give up those organisational, curricula, and pedagogical practices which produce inequity-creating human behaviours. For example, by choosing to adopt the educational philosophies favoured by Australian Aborigines, contemporary societies could benefit greatly from their young developing a strong sense of responsibility to community. In the Indigenous learning context, competitive and individualistic behaviours are highly disapproved of – instead, each child is encouraged to enhance their strongest personal qualities so that they can use them to make a valuable contribution to the entire clan. Additionally, because Aboriginal learning occurs in an holistic way (as an inseparable part of everyday survival, artistic, and spiritual activities), all clan members are, inevitably, important participants in the educational process. Thus, age and status-based hierarchies typical of Western bureaucratic institutions like schools are absent from the Indigenous learning process – as such, cooperation and community activity are modelled for Aboriginal children, while inequitable distributions of power and control are minimised. Finally, as Aboriginal children develop the necessary skills for survival in nomadic societies, they also learn the fundamentals of sharing material possessions and functioning without the acquisition of large amounts of land, money, or weaponry. In this way, then, Aboriginal forms of education discourage the emergence of social conditions that can generate massive inequities between people (both within and across groups). Many Aboriginal Elders believe that humans will face serious problems when they become overly concerned with material things, as the extended family should always be the greater priority. Therefore, a key way that schools could address the challenge of reducing widespread violence, war, and unequal relations between peoples is to abandon the industrial models of education that are increasingly globally dominant and, instead, allow community-based styles of Indigenous learning to flourish.

Summary of the Environmental and Social Benefits of Dominant Australian Aboriginal Ideologies and Practices

Overall, then, the ideologies and practices of the traditional kinship clans of Aboriginal Australia provide a clear indication as to how greater forms of ecological sustainability, peace, and social equity can be achieved in the contemporary world. With their holistic style of education that emphasises respect for nature, peaceful intra- and inter-clan relations, and responsibility to community, the Aboriginal peoples of Australia could certainly offer Western schools a workable model for how children can be shaped into adults who are not seeking high levels of wealth, power, or status, and who both care for their environment and the well-being of their kith and kin. It is only due to their extraordinary ignorance, arrogance, and completely unfounded sense of superiority (that is, given the extremely serious global-scale problems that they have actually generated), that the vast majority of Westerners possess a fundamentally false belief that the Western education system is the only form of 'real' education in existence and, thus, it must be spread to all parts of the world for the supposed 'benefit' of everybody. Ultimately, then, (industrial-style) schools may find that the best response to the current civilisational challenge is to abandon all buildings and the teaching of Western forms of science, numeracy, and written literacy, and instead allow Indigenous learning styles (and hence ideologies and cultural practices) to flourish in natural, community-based environments. Indeed, since their methods of survival already exist, have been developed in accordance with local environmental contexts, and have actually been proven to work over the course of tens of thousands of years, it is Indigenous models of education (unique to each regional landscape) that provide the simplest, most logical, and guaranteed ways of achieving sustainability, relative peace, and greater forms of equity, and thus the creation of a eutopian, rather than dystopian, reality for the planet and humanity as a whole.

*A brief comparison of the myriad global problems generated by the spread of Western societies, in opposition to the great benefits of - or solutions offered by - traditional Aboriginal ideologies and cultural practices is featured in the chart on the following pages.

[NB While the author of this book does have extensive personal experience of living and working with various Indigenous peoples and communities across the land currently known as Australia, the information featured in this chapter has actually been drawn from, or influenced by, materials written by both Indigenous and non-Indigenous peoples (including anthropologists). Please refer to the extensive list of relevant resources in the Bibliography, and especially texts like *Elders: Wisdom from Australia's Indigenous Leaders* (edited by Peter McConchie) and Tyson Yunkaporta's *Sand Talk: How Indigenous Thinking Can Save the World* for primary source explanations of traditional Indigenous models of education. Please also see the Acknowledgement at the start of this text as recognition that the author is aware that her daily practices (including the independent writing of this book) may, unintentionally, have far-reaching consequences of a negative nature for Indigenous peoples. The author's long-term personal commitment is to invest in strategies that will bring greater forms of equity to Indigenous peoples, as well as the revitalisation of traditional ideologies and practices that will be of benefit to the environment and greater humanity. She is aware of the complexities around concerns of non-Indigenous people (like her) misinterpreting and misappropriating Indigenous knowledges, however attempted representation of them still seems to be essential.]

WESTERN / GLOBAL SOCIETY PROBLEMS	ABORIGINAL SOCIETY SOLUTIONS
x High levels of obesity due to lack of regular exercise and dependency on processed (chemical-heavy) junk foods, sugar, caffeine, fat, salt, etc.	+ Extremely nutritious diet (lean meat, native fruits, nuts, water, etc.) and regular forms of exercise (long-distance walking).
x High levels of stress and subsequent addictions to alcohol, drugs, gambling, prescribed medications (anti-depressants), shopping (materialism), cigarettes, etc.	+ Absence of stress-related diseases and enjoyment of good psychological health without addictions to life-destroying behaviours and artificial substances.
x Dependency on highly dangerous forms of weaponry (guns, chemical agents, drones, nuclear bombs, etc.) and regular engagement in large-scale wars on foreign lands (World Wars 1 and 2, the wars in Korea, Vietnam, Iraq, Afghanistan, etc.) to maintain Western power and global dominance.	+ Long-term and widespread peace, with a complete absence of weaponry designed to kill other human beings in large numbers, and with an ongoing commitment to interconnectedness by creating harmonious ties with all kith, kin, and neighbouring clans.
x Increasing engagement in spiritually-harmful competitive behaviours (leading to a lack of quality sleep) due to growing disconnection from nature and intuition, as well as an over-reliance on environment-damaging technologies, practices, and behaviours.	+ Intimate, lifelong connection with nature; low reliance on artificial and polluting forms of technology; and strong spiritual understanding of life, with cooperative behaviours (sharing), dream-life, and intuition greatly valued.

x Imperial spread of British- / Euro-centric educational, economic, political, religious, and legal systems that promote class-based hierarchies, divisions, injustice, and discrimination. High levels of political corruption, with widespread lack of transparency and accountability.	+ Maintenance of social practices most suited to the local landscape (and not arrogantly spread to other peoples and locations). Participatory democracy reliant on evolving forms of consensus - no leaders, but all Elders (of both genders) respected for their wisdom.
x High levels of disease / illness and widespread dependency on artificial and environment-damaging (over-packaged, factory-produced) medicines.	+ Healthy and long lives enjoyed due to isolation from most forms of disease (including the common cold) and cures based on natural sources / psychology.
x Relentless and ongoing deforestation; intensive agriculture; mining; construction; urban sprawl; manufacture of material products; and environmental pollution in the name of capitalism and consumerism.	+ Operation of non-monetary lifestyles that emphasise custodianship (rather than ownership) of land, and environmentally-friendly forms of artistic life and survival (for example, via gathering) over materialism.
x Children treated as forms of 'human capital' in the Western education system – with the primary aim being to inculcate students via written forms of literacy and scientific, technological, and mathematical processes that seek to control nature (thereby encouraging them to exploit the environment for maximum material gain).	+ Utilisation of an holistic education system where children are not separated from their kith and kin or nature, and where wisdom and ethical and spiritual knowledge (rather than mere 'cleverness' and control) are learnt via storytelling and Dreaming processes that are interwoven with survival.

x High rates of crime (especially property theft and violence) and incarceration (particularly of already economically and racially disadvantaged peoples in disproportionate numbers).	+ No existence of police, jails, or artificial legal processes run by external strangers. Crime minimised via operation of a non-materialistic society and a philosophy of sharing everything.
x Belief in increasing populations (through breeding or immigration) for economic reasons, rather than emphasis on maintaining an appropriately-sized population for the availability of resources (for example, underground water supplies) on a given landscape.	+ Maintenance of small populations that operate in a nomadic manner, ensuring that survival occurs in areas of seasonal plenty while other parts of the land are given an opportunity to replenish. Emphasis on conservation and sustainability rather than resource exhaustion.
x Focus on short-term survival and ambitious and greedy behaviours that serve individualism and ensure the wealth and power of only a few. Highly technological forms of industry imposed on a local and international scale, and exploitation of resources and peoples (via lowly-paid human labour) in foreign locations to maximise profit. High levels of disregard for overseas peoples who are suffering because of the actions of Westerners (for example, Africans who are starving due to desertification caused by climate change resulting from Western carbon emissions).	+ Focus on long-term survival through a belief that humans are an inseparable part of nature who must honour their bond with the environment through deep respect and a set of responsibilities to the land and its creatures (who themselves have rights). Moderate resource use in annually visited and cared for local areas (all within walking distance) ensures low destructive impact on the land.

x Devaluing of women and their roles and knowledges (for example, child rearing, oral forms of communication to maintain close family and community ties, etc.). Many forms of Feminism that focus on women becoming like Western males in order to achieve status, power, and wealth in wider society (that is, a sacrificing of domestic life in order to make money and achieve 'respect').	+ Women's roles and knowledges considered to be of equal importance as men's ('secret women's business' valued by the entire clan, and respected Elders being both males and females). Female (quiet, oral) ways of communicating preferenced by both genders – for example, children are gently teased (rather than smacked in a violent manner) in order to modify problematic behaviours.
x Groundless belief in 'superiority' of Western culture (for example, Christianity, representative 'democracy', science, etc.), hence feeling of 'civilising justification' when engaging in colonial acts of invasion, massacring, assimilation, and genocide of Indigenous lands, peoples, and cultures. Refusal to change mode of survival even when shown widescale destruction caused by Westerners.	+ Belief in cooperation for survival and an emphasis on community and behaviours that unify (not divide). Equal forms of sharing ensure that hierarchies, the power of a few, and individualised forms of ambition are discouraged. Belief in taking care of Country on a local level prevents invasions of other lands (and thus destruction of other cultures).

*In the 1970s and 1980s, the Australian federal government adopted the policies of Integration, Self-Determination, and Self-Management with respect to Aboriginal peoples. In 1991, Reconciliation became the official policy. Many would justifiably argue, however, that none of these policies have been very successful, as Indigenous peoples have continued to be subjected to extensive government interference via forcibly imposed Western education, legal, and economic systems.

CHAPTER 4
PROPOSED LEGAL ACTION FOR EDUCATION SYSTEM TRANSFORMATION

Potential Legal Cases to Force Education System Transformation

Governments that benefit significantly from the highly inequitable, nature-destroying status quo, and which therefore refuse to transform existing education systems and institutions, can potentially face legal action to make them accountable for the continued harm (to children and local and global environments) they are generating. Legal action could also be taken against socioeconomically privileged politicians and bureaucrats (such as Ministers for Education and Director-Generals of Departments of Education) to force them to provide greater educational equity and support to currently disadvantaged students in schools (for example, children from Indigenous and Culturally and Linguistically Diverse Backgrounds).

Ultimately, Westerners continue to lack fundamental knowledge of, and respect for, Indigenous cultures and peoples because they are exposed to a highly racist and imperialistically-imposed education system that still foregrounds Eurocentric bodies of knowledge. To eliminate discriminatory and anti-environment beliefs, attitudes, and behaviours, the curriculum, assessment, and pedagogical approaches of the dominant education system must be transformed. Just as Eddie (Koiki) Mabo and Martin Luther King, Jr. used legal processes to modify a racist status quo (on matters of land and politics), action can be taken to ensure an equitable representation of Indigenous, Holistic, Multicultural, and Futures knowledges and pedagogies in all contemporary educational contexts. Potential legal cases could thus include action against Federal and State Governments (and their employees) for use of the Western education system as an apparatus for the continued *genocide* of Indigenous cultures; for causing various forms of physical, psychological, emotional, and ideological *harm* to children (including teaching them how to commit life-threatening acts of ecocide); and for the enacting of *arbitrary prejudice* against Indigenous knowledges and peoples of non-Western backgrounds.

All states and countries operating under Western (or Western-style) law have codes that can be utilised to make those in positions of power accountable for the various forms of harm and destruction being exacted by Western educational institutions (such as schools) on wider society, humanity, and the environment. Some key legal concepts are outlined below (check online for each particular state's / country's related laws and the civil or criminal action they can give rise to).

Parens Patriae and Duty of Person Who Has Care of Child

According to these concepts, governments and their employees (including education system ministers, bureaucrats, administrators, and teachers) have a legal obligation to ensure the welfare of children. In Western and Westernised schools all throughout the world, children are, however, being exposed to inherently violent, environment-damaging, and inequity-creating ideologies, and many suffer great stress and lowered forms of self-esteem through being repeatedly tested, graded, ranked, and labelled as 'low achievers' (that is, failures) when forcibly assessed on their ability to master fundamentally racist, classist, and otherwise biased Western bodies of knowledge. In one section of the *Criminal Code Act* from Queensland (Australia), the duty of every person who has care of a child under 16 years (including any adult in charge of a child, whether or not the person has lawful custody) is legally required to "take the precautions that are reasonable in all the circumstances to avoid danger to the child's life, health or safety…and he or she is held to have caused any consequences that result to the life and health of the child because of any omission to perform that duty" (286).

More broadly, a breach of duty of care is legally defined as negligent or careless conduct, or failure to act, of a person who owes a duty of care to another and who fails to maintain the standard of care necessary to fulfil that duty. Any child or student suffering from emotional or psychological harm as a result of substandard pedagogies in schools (such as a teacher bullying a pupil for performing poorly on a standardised exam that tests only written forms of literacy) can therefore argue that their mental health has been put in *danger*. Where a child may attempt suicide in order to avoid the various high stresses associated with schooling processes, an additional case can be made that their life has been put in *danger*. Given the extraordinarily high suicide rates of young people in many Australian communities, there is a valid argument that the efforts of teachers to repeatedly lower students' self-esteem by forcing them to learn environment-damaging Western practices (and then frequently labelling culturally diverse pupils as 'low achievers' when they cannot perform such acts) constitutes a form of cultural genocide that, in legal terms, can be classified as a *danger to safety*. From a legal perspective, school administrators and teachers who repeatedly yell at, berate, or negatively label children can also be accused of *emotional abuse* (ill-treating, or exposing or subjecting a child to behaviour that causes psychological harm to the child, whether or not with the consent of the child). [The outstanding documentary *Keeping Hope* compassionately explores the fact that the Kimberley region of Western Australian has the highest rate of suicide per capita in the world (including very large numbers of Indigenous children and adolescents who have taken their own life).]

Abuse of Office and Refusal by Public Officer to Perform Duty

Engagement in acts of *arbitrary prejudice* (or a failure to act impartially) by public officers (government employees / public servants) can constitute a breach of law. Thus, education system employees engaged in implementing Western-centric curriculum, pedagogy, and assessment programmes which pose an *arbitrary prejudice* against, or form of *detriment* to, culturally diverse students can potentially face charges. According to the aforementioned *Criminal Code Act,* "Any person who, being employed in the public service, does or directs to be done, in abuse of the authority of the person's office, an arbitrary act prejudicial to the rights of another is guilty of a misdemeanour, and is liable to imprisonment for 2 years" (92). In Queensland (Australia), teachers are required by various professional documents (including syllabuses and policies) to embed Aboriginal and Torres Strait Islander perspectives into their educational practice, however thousands of educators are simply not doing this at all (let alone regularly) and, as such, they are engaging in acts of *arbitrary prejudice* against their Indigenous students (ensuring that the latter are more likely to fail by continuously being assessed on less familiar Western skills and knowledges). Where teachers are knowingly and deliberately not embedding Indigenous perspectives in their units, their actions could be construed as a refusal by public officer to perform duty and, according to the aforementioned *Criminal Code Act,* "Any person who, being employed in the public service, or as an officer of any court or tribunal, perversely and without lawful excuse omits or refuses to do any act which it is his or her duty to do by virtue of his or her employment is guilty of a misdemeanour, and is liable to imprisonment for 2 years, and to be fined at the discretion of the court" (200).

Neglect and Educational Negligence / Malpractice

For those students who are regularly not having their educational needs properly evaluated or adequately met, either Western governments and education departments (as a whole) or schools and teachers (as individuals) can be made legally accountable for various forms of neglect, negligence, or malpractice. In a general legal sense, *neglect* can be defined as a failure to perform a duty or obligation; or to omit or fail to do something through carelessness or negligence. *Educational negligence* or *educational malpractice* is, meanwhile, more specifically regarded as incompetent teaching of a student or negligent evaluation of a student's educational needs. The extensive educational needs of students from a range of marginalised backgrounds are regularly improperly evaluated, and subsequently catered for in a highly inadequate or negligent way in contemporary schools. The broader funding-related neglect often occurs at a systemic level, with essential resources and support services frequently being inappropriately or unfairly distributed. Meanwhile, poorly trained, incompetent, and intellectually underqualified education system employees further compound academic underachievement through acts of malpractice (especially in relation to disadvantaged students who have the greatest educational needs).

Other Legal Options

Other legal concepts which may be of use in making government and education system employees accountable for acts of harm include:
- Ministerial Responsibility;
- Misconduct in Relation to Public Office;
- Breach of Statutory Duty / Disobedience to Statute Law;
- Racial Discrimination; and
- Unfairly Prejudicial or Unfairly Discriminatory Conduct.

It should also be noted that legal provisions exist for concerned citizens (independently or in conjunction) to bring direct action against all public sector individuals engaging in criminal behaviours (that is, without assistance from negligent police or crime, misconduct, and corruption regulatory bodies). For instance, the power of private citizens to apprehend offenders exists at both common law and under legislation, and a private informant is a person who commences a prosecution and is not doing so in the capacity of a police officer or other government employee [generally, any person can commence a prosecution for an offence of a public nature]. As well, it is possible to advocate for public interest litigation, which is a suit commenced in which a plaintiff is able to establish a special interest in the subject matter, notwithstanding that the subject matter also involves issues of public interest; a suit brought by the Attorney-General as a representative of the Crown with responsibility for protecting the public interest; or a relator action, where the Attorney-General has granted a fiat to a private individual to commence a suit in the name of the Attorney-General in a matter involving an issue of public interest (that is, to establish the unlawfulness of an action or to restrain a threatened breach of law enacted in the public interest).

*Legal definitions featured in this chapter have been taken from the *Concise Australian Legal Dictionary* published by Butterworths. Definitions for additional legal terms, phrases, and concepts of potential relevance for civil or criminal action [see below] can also be sourced from this text or any reputable Western legal dictionary.
- Complicity;
- Continuing Offence;
- Corrupt Conduct;
- Corruption of Public Morals;
- Criminal Negligence;
- Due Diligence;
- Duty of Skill;
- Duty to Disclose;
- Emotional Abuse;
- Emotional Distress;
- Employer's Duty of Care;
- Endangerment;
- Gross Negligence;
- Hardship;
- Harass;
- Hinder;

- Imperitia culpae adnumeratur (lack of skill is regarded as fault);
- Improper Conduct;
- Incompetence;
- Intentional Act;
- Interest reipublicae ne maleficia remaneant impunita (it is in the interest of the state that wrongdoing does not remain unpunished);
- Intimidation;
- Knowingly Concerned In;
- Likelihood of Risk;
- Mala praxis (bad conduct – injury caused by neglect or want of skill);
- Negligent Misrepresentation;
- Non-Delegable Duty;
- Oppressive,
- Pain and Suffering;
- Professional Misconduct;
- Professional Negligence;
- Professional Responsibility;
- Qui facit per alium facit per se (the rationale behind the doctrine of vicarious liability by which an employer or principal is responsible for damage caused by his or her employee's negligent acts committed within the scope of the employee's authority);
- Qui tacet consentire videtur (one who is silent is regarded as consenting);
- Real Risk;
- Reckless Indifference;
- Secondary Participant;
- Serious or Wilful Misconduct;
- Statutory Duty;
- Statutory Prohibition;
- Unlawful Act;
- Victimisation; and
- Welfare Principle.

PART 2:

EMPOWERING AGENTS OF POSITIVE WORLD CHANGE THROUGH KEY PROCESSES, CONCEPTS, GUIDANCE, AND INSIGHTS

Chapter 5: Empowering Agents of Positive World Change Through Life Purpose Establishment / Clarification Processes
- Key Questions to Establish / Clarify Life Purpose
- A Visionary Life
- Pursuing a Higher Cause / Greater Purpose
- Individual Identity and Life Passion
- Universal Plan

Chapter 6: Empowering Agents of Positive World Change Through Multidisciplinary Conceptions of 'Infinity' and 'Unity'
- Meaning of the Word 'Infinity'
- An Overarching Definition of Infinity
- Traditional Indigenous Worldviews
- Acausal Parallelisms (Synchronicities)
- Quantum Mechanics
- Oneness: One Wave Function and Unified Field Theory
- The Interconnectedness of All Particles: Entanglement, Superposition, and Neuroscientific / Metaphysical Explanations for Instant Manifestations
- Other Evidence of a Living Universe
- Many-Worlds Theory (The Multiverse)
- Consciousness Is All There Is

Chapter 7: Empowering Agents of Positive World Change Through Various Forms of Guidance

- Myths, Archetypes, and The Collective Unconscious
- Dreams, Fantasies, and Astral Travel
- Signs and Symbols
- Guides - Imaginal Guides - Nature Guides and Power Animals - Shamanic Journeys
- Earth Guides - Anam Caras and Soul Mates - Twin Souls - Twin Flames - The Future of Love – Lightworkers, Spiritual Messengers, and Cosmic Messengers

Chapter 8: Empowering Agents of Positive World Change Through Various Forms of Insight

- Intuition – Ways to Develop Skills of Intuition – Activities for Accessing Intuitive Information
- Telepathy and Remote Viewing
- Psychic Awareness and Mediumship – Becoming Open to Receiving Psychic Information
- The Akashic Field and The Akashic Records – Becoming Open to Guidance From The Akashic Records
- Forms of Awakening
- The Universal Laws
- Soul Lessons and Life Purpose

*As noted in the Preface, Part 2 contains information from a wide range of theoretical perspectives. Even if readers are sceptical about some of the ideas, there may still be key concepts that prove to be useful in the personal empowerment process, and which will ultimately assist individuals in working to create a better world. When evaluating various strategies ('cutting-edge ideas'), it is wise to keep an open mind and find commonalities and unity in diverse beliefs (especially if they are able to bring great benefit to the world). Additional research into key approaches is highly recommended [refer to Appendix B and the Bibliography at the end of the book].

CHAPTER 5
EMPOWERING AGENTS OF POSITIVE WORLD CHANGE THROUGH LIFE PURPOSE ESTABLISHMENT / CLARIFICATION PROCESSES

Key Questions to Establish / Clarify Life Purpose

By providing answers to the following questions, individuals and entire groups can feel a greater sense of empowerment as they consciously establish, clarify, or confirm what positive change they most want to bring to the world.

1. If you had unlimited power, what one thing would you do to improve the world?
2. What are the major issues you think humanity needs to focus on?
3. What issue are you most passionate about? What higher cause do you feel compelled to give your greatest energy to for the betterment of humanity and the planet? What important topic can most sustain your interest, attention, excitement, enthusiasm, and investment of time and effort (action) in a happy, positive, joyous, or loving way (making you feel both alive and empowered)? [NB Your primary focus may differ during progressive life phases, but eventually separate pursuits may converge so that you can achieve something significant.]
4. What preferred future do you envision in relation to your chosen issue?
5. ESTABLISHING / CLARIFYING / CONFIRMING
   What are you on planet Earth to do? What is your life calling / mission / soul purpose?
   - Personal Level:
   - Local / Regional Level:
   - State Level:
   - National Level:
   - Global Level:
6. (a) How long do you have to achieve your core purpose?
   (b) Where should you be to achieve it?
   (c) What opportunities / resources / help do you need?
   (d) Who do you need to collaborate with?
7. What are your major values, ideals, skills, talents, and strengths? (What do you believe in and what are you good at?)

In what way can you best make an important contribution to the betterment of the world?
8. What are you willing to sacrifice / transcend to fulfil your life purpose? [Ego, Status, Money, Materialism, Addictions, etc.]
9. Who inspires you? Who are your heroes and why?

A Visionary Life

Many psychological studies have found that people have a much greater sense of self-worth, and consequently happiness, when they are committed to a higher cause. Identifying with a meaningful greater purpose also dramatically increases an individual's ability to cope with challenging situations. Such resilience then promotes an inclination to positively interpret 'obstacles' on the life path as opportunities for learning and growth. According to Marc Allen (*A Visionary Life*), an individual should envision a preferred future for humanity and the environment in order to lead a more purposeful life. The focus for creating a eutopian future could be on devising strategies to increase social justice for disadvantaged groups; promoting global peace and harmony; doing healing work on the body, mind, and soul level; or working on issues of ecological protection, sustainability, and environmental stewardship.

Establishing a clear vision inspires enthusiasm, as well as a joyful investment of time, energy, and effort. For this reason, it is important that individuals pursue what they actually *like* doing, as it is then easier to stay motivated and engaged. Boredom may be an indication that all has been learnt from utilising certain approaches and methods, and it is either time to try new ways of pursuing key goals, or to shift attention to other higher causes that are equally important. Bringing about noble advancement in one area can also indirectly generate significant progress for other causes (locally, globally, and across time periods). Indeed, there can often be complex intergenerational and cross-geographical interconnections at play that it is not always possible to be consciously aware of. For instance, in his efforts to bring legal action that would ensure African-Americans were properly politically enfranchised, Martin Luther King, Jr. was heavily influenced by the peaceful strategies favoured by Mahatma Gandhi in India decades prior. There are no set 'rules' for how to bring about processes of positive change – it quite often takes people working at multiple levels across all sectors of society, and even transformations that appear rapid may have taken very long periods of time to orchestrate. Even if it is not possible to see the direct impact of individual actions, others may be influenced in indirect or long-term ways. When electing to do anything in the world, what is of most importance is that all intentions are aligned with higher qualities like love, tolerance, and compassion, and that the activities being engaged in generate passion and energy.

Ultimately, after determining the higher cause that brings greatest inspiration, it is possible to work independently or with other like-minded individuals to create a preferred reality. In working to make the world a better place, determination and commitment are always recognised at a higher level, and both inspiration and assistance are brought to those who are positive and open to receiving support.

Pursuing a Higher Cause / Greater Purpose

Individuals who are prepared to move beyond the ego state, and to operate beyond lower-level energies like competition and greed (which are still ingrained in societies that are addicted to hierarchies and materialism), may find themselves receiving significant forms of guidance and support from higher sources. For example, people who are prepared to devote their lives to a greater purpose often report an increase in seeing important signs and symbols; having meaningful dreams and visions; experiencing frequent synchronicities; hearing messages from guides; and enjoying enhanced telepathic and psychic abilities. Guiding information is typically presented in forms that a person finds familiar, as well as in ways which make them feel most comfortable. For example, one person may prefer to receive insights from books, song lyrics, or films, while another may find that they can communicate directly with otherworldly guides. All forms of guidance can work to empower and assist those who are working to create positive world transformation.

Those who open themselves up to be a channel for higher energy can also find themselves on the path to generating beneficial world change. Musicians, writers, actors, and visual artists frequently report being filled with some kind of 'divine inspiration', as though certain songs, books, performances, and artworks simply create themselves (or 'pour out' of the channel in a very rapid and unimpeded manner). A large number of scientists and inventors throughout history have also attested to having some kind of unexpected 'Eureka!' moment - often at times when they were not even consciously focused on solving a problem. The extraordinary story of early twentieth century Indian mathematician Ramanujan (whose life is explored in the book and film *The Man Who Knew Infinity*) is just one example of a man who was undoubtedly channelling information from a higher source. When Ramanujan prayed to the Goddess Namagiri (Lakshmi), many previously elusive advanced mathematical theorems simply appeared in his head (without accompanying proofs), and most of these have only been properly understood and successfully applied since his death. Ultimately, for people who are open-minded, it is clear that information, support, guidance, and help can come in a myriad of ways to promote the creation of positive world change.

Individual Identity and Life Passion

At the basic personality level, most people are comfortable with identifying those characteristics that form their individual identities. This includes the skills and talents that seem to come 'naturally', or which they are especially motivated to spend time developing in a particular life. Special interests can steadily evolve over the course of a lifetime, or what provided stimulation in childhood can re-emerge as important passions at key junctures in adulthood (perhaps after pursuing other crucial forms of knowledge in a tangential way). What each person does in a single life can, indeed, be a tapestry of interwoven threads. Ideas, experiences, and actions that may have originally seemed irrelevant, challenging, or disparate, can prove to be deeply and profoundly interconnected when an individual comes to a conscious awareness of their greater life purpose.

In the course of realising one's planetary agenda, Shakti Gawain's key message in *Living in the Light* is to 'follow the energy' and bring a higher purpose to those activities that most hold attention or cause the greatest excitement. Gawain advocates for people to constantly tune in to energy and to where it wants to go, then to follow or move with it. By developing greater awareness of how energy can be channelled, blocked, or controlled, an individual may willingly and consciously choose to surrender to the energy within, and thereby allow greater forms of power to flow through them (this is because energy equates to power). Intuition is one way in which a person can internally feel the movement of energy and allow it to direct them. Gawain also encourages individuals to be exactly where they want to be at every moment: to be where the energy is greatest for them, doing what they want to do, and working to channel all that is able to positively assist others. She explains that energy flows 'through', 'out', and 'in' - every single person receives energy from, and gives energy to, other people. As well, a higher power can create via (or do work through) individuals who are open to channelling its energy. Ultimately, entering into situations where the energy is intensely positive and expansive can accelerate healing, awareness, and growth: it can inspire, support, and push people to move forward on their personal journeys. In conjunction with harnessing energy, articulating the values, virtues, and ideals that matter most to an individual can enhance decision-making and clarify life direction.

Thus, by coming to know the self intimately and, subsequently, pursuing a greater life purpose, it is possible for individuals to become more personally empowered, and so better able to generate positive change in the world.

Universal Plan

An increasingly dominant notion in much New Age literature is that all humans formulated a 'life blueprint' before incarnating on planet Earth, and, in fact, every person has agreed to have a number of specific experiences as a way of learning lessons across multiple lives. As an extension of this is the idea that it is not just the individual that is growing in wisdom, but all humans are actually a manifestation of one consciousness, with each 'life' simply being a projection of that consciousness. Further to this belief is that all individuals are part of an intelligent living universe with a greater universal plan, of which there are varying levels of awareness. Young souls may play out their life dramas in a largely unconscious way, consistently subscribing to 'unenlightened' beliefs in suffering, while old souls (those who have had many life incarnations or manifestations) are able to transcend the ego state in a more conscious and joyous way. Such conceptions provide a pathway to better comprehending the role that all humans play in a more expansive reality.

In *The Light-Worker's Companion*, Amanda Guggenheimer explains that a soul can request to incarnate for evolutionary purposes; elect a particular life in order to clear karma; or be chosen / asked to volunteer for the fulfilment of different assignments on Earth. She outlines a number of roles that humans may embrace in any given life. For example, some people may devote themselves to bringing hope, faith, inspiration, awareness, or support to others (using vision to 'light the way' for wider humanity). She further identifies individuals who operate as 'circuit breakers' in their ability to consciously transcend negative and damaging patterns, cycles, and behaviours. These people are also able to help others move beyond intergenerational trauma. Meanwhile, those she refers to as 'way showers' are souls who make major contributions to the world as a result of their great personal integrity. They are often committed to larger environmental or humanitarian causes, and will take any risk - such as being persecuted, jailed, or killed - to achieve justice, regardless of how they may be judged in this lifetime. It is possible for an individual to take on different roles at key points, or to even embody multiple roles simultaneously.

In coming to a deep understanding of who they are on the planet, Guggenheimer claims that individuals can go through several 'activating the blueprint' and 'ascension' processes. Periods of self-discovery and awakening can be achieved via acts of healing (such as of anger, depression, or sabotage) and spiritual growth (including by regularly meditating, reading metaphysical materials, or attending personal development workshops). Requesting assistance, being open to alternatives, and trusting guidance from higher energies (such as from dreams) can all lead to growing consciousness of one's greater life purpose. When an individual takes responsibility for all their beliefs, choices, actions, and emotions, they can also feel an increased sense of liberation, freedom, and clarity. According to Guggenheimer, seeing life from a different perspective can further result in people creating (or attracting) fewer situations of pain, suffering, and chaos, and instead lead to them manifesting greater forms of joy, abundance, and inner power. In a more psychologically positive and emotionally healthy state, individuals are then better able to assist humanity and the world in accordance with a greater universal plan that is unfolding (or which may still be formulating).

CHAPTER 6
EMPOWERING AGENTS OF POSITIVE WORLD CHANGE THROUGH MULTIDISCIPLINARY CONCEPTIONS OF 'INFINITY' AND 'UNITY'

Accepting that the potential of humans and the human mind is Infinite allows anyone to embrace limitless possibilities and attract unlimited opportunities. Embracing a personal conception of 'limitlessness' is phenomenally empowering for any individual who is committed to generating positive world change. This chapter explores multidisciplinary approaches to conceptions of 'Infinity' and 'Unity', and how motivated changemakers can draw on different cultural ideologies and a range of academic theories and findings to manifest outer world realities that once would have been perceived as 'miracles'. As any *Star Wars* fan knows, developing the skill of being able to harness energy ('The Force') can result in significant personal power that must be used responsibly and for purposes of the greater good.

Meaning of the Word 'Infinity'

The English word 'infinity' is derived from the Latin word 'infinitas' (meaning 'unboundedness'), which originated from the Greek word 'apeiros' (meaning 'without end', 'endless', or 'limitless').

An Overarching Definition of Infinity: The Paradox of Infinity as a Concept Beyond 'Space' and 'Time' Whilst Commonly Being Defined in Spatial and Temporal Terms

A strong argument is that Infinity is not actually about space or time – in fact, it is about being beyond space and time, or the *non-existence* of space and time. Where 'space' and 'time' are simply Earth-bound (especially Western) constructs, then Infinity cannot be defined in terms of either concept. Another common notion is that a proper comprehension of Infinity can only occur through direct physical experience. Whilst thinking and communicating in English, however, the following spatially- and temporally-related terms and phrases offer some level of understanding of the abstract idea of Infinity through linguistic means. Infinity as:

- unlimited / limitless / limitlessness / no limit (or limits) / without limits / no limitations;
- without boundaries / unbounded / unboundedness / increasing without bound / boundless;
- exceedingly or immeasurably great;
- immense / immensity;
- expansion / expansiveness;
- no end / endless / endlessness / without end / never ending (in both spatial and temporal terms);
- eternal / eternity;
- everlasting; and
- forever.

In purely definitional terms, the word 'infinity' can more exclusively be regarded as a concept related to 'space' and the word 'eternity' as a concept related to 'time', however the concept of Infinity is so often regarded as being relevant to 'space' *and* 'time' that both ideas will be explored in this section. The notion that Infinity is beyond (or about the non-existence of) space and time will also be foregrounded. [*See Appendix B for a detailed exploration of how the word 'Infinity' appears in multiple languages, disciplines, and spiritual beliefs, suggesting that it is a universal (and, thus, potentially unifying) concept.]

Traditional Indigenous Worldviews

There is extensive evidence across the world that traditionally-oriented Indigenous peoples have access to insights and abilities that most contemporary peoples do not (or, perhaps, that the latter are simply no longer capable of due to a disconnection from nature and key ideologies). In his landmark book *Sand Talk: How Indigenous Thinking Can Save the World*, Tyson Yunkaporta explores traditional Australian Aboriginal conceptions of Infinity and Unity in a myriad of ways. He notes that for Australian Indigenous peoples, 'space' and 'time' are not separate concepts and everything (kinship, the seasons, the sky) is perceived as moving in endless cycles. For Aboriginal peoples, time is not linear (as it is for Westerners): 'past', 'present', and 'future' are actually all one time, one place (there is no 'beginning', 'middle', or 'end' as there is in the Western worldview). Yunkaporta also explains that traditional Aboriginal peoples do not believe that humans ever die, but rather that everybody goes back to Country. Indeed, nothing can ever be created or destroyed because regeneration and renewal are themselves Infinite. As is the case for Indigenous peoples around the world, notions of interconnectedness are central to traditional Australian Aboriginal ways of relating to other people; the land and features of the landscape; trees and plants; birds and animals; the weather; and everything there is. Such beliefs hold amazing potential for agents of positive world change to perceive reality in an expanded and unified way, and to thereby create new opportunities for cultural transformation in highly effective ways.

Acausal Parallelisms (Synchronicities)

Carl Jung's development of theories regarding acausal parallelisms ('synchronicities') provides deep insight into how inner processes can be manifested in the outer world. Experiencing an increased number of synchronicities is actually a fundamental skill that individuals can develop in order to assist them in generating extensive positive change in the world.

According to Jung, synchronicities are occurrences that appear, on the surface, to be a coincidence, but which actually have deep significance and meaning. One explanation for synchronistic events is that they are evidence that an individual is 'on the right track' in terms of how they are interpreting and responding to everyday situations, or that they are taking appropriate life actions at the broader level. Alternatively, synchronicities may occur in order to overtly draw attention to an idea or concept that has not been previously considered. For instance, a person may be feeling suicidal, but then they dream about a ladybug (a sign of good luck) landing on their nose, and the next day they run into a former school friend (who they heard through the grapevine survived a suicide attempt) and, during the course of conversing with the latter, a ladybug lands on their face. There are multiple levels of synchronicity occurring here, and Jung would suggest that the common symbol of good luck and meeting a survivor should be enough to provide the individual with a sense of psychic healing and, thus, allow them to let go of all negative, neurotic, or suicidal thoughts. Ultimately, a synchronicity can be seen as something inner that needs to be expressed (or which must become manifest) in the outer world at a key moment.

By being open to seeking support from, trusting, and working in conjunction with a higher energy (such as Infinity), an individual will be provided with meaningful synchronistic events and guidance on an increasingly frequent basis. According to F. David Peat (*Synchronicity: The Bridge Between Mind and Matter*), it is essential to activate 'the deep forces' of the unconscious mind in order for synchronicities to occur. Since synchronicity is associated with a profound activation of energy within the psyche, the formation of patterns within the unconscious mind will then be accompanied by physical patterns in the outer world. As synchronicities are meaningful arrangements, Peat also believes that they reveal a universe that unfolds according to a hidden, dynamic order. He says that synchronicities depend on individuals detecting a deeper meaning to the patterns and clusterings of the phenomena that are occurring all around them. This can involve seeing the underlying patterns in all environments, situations, events, and interactions or relationships with other people.

In *SynchroDestiny*, Deepak Chopra makes the concept even more relevant to agents of positive world change by arguing that following synchronicities allows an individual to fully realise their life purpose and ultimate destiny (he also asserts that synchronicities become more frequent if they are being paid proper heed to). For instance, a person may set a higher purpose intention that they want to bring legal action to force the government to make school curricula more focused on sustainability and environmental stewardship, so they read a large number of books about educational theory and the law. They then attend a local film festival where they meet a young woman who is making a documentary about ecological issues, and who needs assistance with many legal matters that she is dealing with in the course of completing her production (such legal concepts and language now being readily comprehended as a result of the individual's previous research). In the course of working together, many synchronicities, instant manifestations, and telepathic moments are experienced, and it becomes increasingly clear that helping the filmmaker secure major distribution for her documentary will result in generating enough profit to fund the legal cases required to transform the education system. In the course of interacting with each other, both parties are forced to face a series of difficult challenges (in which a number of karmic life themes emerge to be resolved), but by trusting the guidance from the synchronicities, an extremely productive lifelong working partnership with the documentarian is eventually established.

Deepak Chopra would agree that the path of SynchroDestiny is not always easy on the surface (or everyday) level, but it is highly important, purposeful, and ultimately rewarding. The Jungian individuation process is also about moving the ego into service of the higher self, and this can lead to an increased number of synchronicities presenting themselves on the road to destiny and actively working to create a better world.

Quantum Mechanics

Quantum theories also provide clues as to how human potential may indeed be 'limitless' in nature – and how agents of positive world change can therefore use quantum ideas as a means of personal empowerment.

Through the means of quantum physics, many Westerners are able to grasp ideas about Unity and Infinity in the form of a number of scientific concepts. Quantum mechanics is the study of how the universe behaves at the smallest levels of reality - that is, the nature and behaviour of matter and energy on the molecular, atomic, and subatomic levels. The laws of classical physics are stable and predictable, and they govern how humans perceive everyday reality at the larger (macroscopic) level. Studies in the field of quantum mechanics have demonstrated, however, that these laws do not operate in the same consistent way at the microscopic level. For instance, many quantum physicists have posited time and space theories that collapse traditional scientific and Western notions of these concepts. One proposition is that, at the quantum level, there is no linear or 'forward moving' form of time – things can actually go backwards (in reverse) or be timeless. Many other key theories developed by quantum physicists provide a conceptual path for greater comprehension of concepts like Unity and Infinity.

Oneness: One Wave Function and Unified Field Theory

The fundamental assertion of classical physics is that all particles are located in one particular place. At the quantum level, however, physicists have discovered that particles can appear to be in only one location when observed, but they are actually part of a wave function when they are not being observed (giving rise to Heisenberg's Uncertainty Principle and The Observer Effect). This apparent wave-particle duality (in which a 'particle' is *both* a particle and a wave) suggests that, in reality, particles are always unified into one quantum state governed by one wave function.

Unified Field Theory claims, then, that reality is characterised by connectivity amongst all things. In other words, there is one wave of information and vibration that gives rise to everything in the universe (The Unified Field). Another proposition is that everything was entangled at the moment of The Big Bang, therefore everything is still touching – 'space' is just a construct, and the idea of there being a 'separation' between objects is merely an illusion. According to the film *What the Bleep Do We Know!?* and the accompanying documentary *Down the Rabbit Hole* (featuring interviews with independent physicist Fred Alan Wolf, and quantum hypotheses of consciousness developed by Stuart Hameroff and Roger Penrose), the deepest level of truth is thus unity – everything is one and there is an invisible connection between all things (including all human souls). Such unity at the most fundamental level of existence can be massively inspiring and empowering for all proponents of positive world transformation, as will become increasingly clear in the following sections.

The Interconnectedness of All Particles: Entanglement, Superposition, and Neuroscientific / Metaphysical Explanations for Instant Manifestations

In accordance with Unified Field Theory, entanglement is the notion that all particles are interconnected, regardless of space (distance) and time. If reality is actually just one wave function that is spread out over all space and time, then no particle is ever localised in one place at one time - *all* locations and times ('past', 'present', and 'future') are *always* accessible. The theory of superposition also asserts that particles can be in *multiple* places at any moment. Further, if places in space are all actually the same (part of the same wave function), then particles can always be co-located (or multi-located).

Entanglement and superposition can, then, be used to explain occurrences that traditional science would once have found difficult to accept. For instance, in *The Conscious Universe*, Dean Radin (from the Institute of Noetic Sciences) argues that what is referred to as 'telepathic' communication may actually be the human mind engaging in a transmission, transfer, or sharing of information while it is in two (or multiple) locations at the same time. Similarly, 'precognition' or 'psychic visions' may actually be the mind localising in both the 'future' and the 'present' at the same time. Quantum mechanics also says that the deeper and smaller one goes, the more energy and power one has, hence why phenomena like instant manifestations (in response to clear and focused intentions) are possible. Joe Dispenza's work in areas of neuroscience (as documented in his book *Becoming Supernatural*) provides growing evidence of the power of the human mind and its ability to engage in acts of 'instant manifestation' – that is, producing external outcomes that some would have previously regarded as 'miracles'. Metaphysical explanations for how negative thinking is able to create disease, and how guided meditation or the placebo effect are able to generate instant healing, are thus completely justified by quantum theory.

In mind-matter interaction, human intention is directly reflected in the external circumstances being generated. Nothing is random - humans are, in fact, creating their own reality all the time, and what is accepted as absolute truth manifests in the individual's life. The film *King Richard* is an extraordinary testament to how Richard Williams developed a clear plan and vision prior to the birth of his daughters (Venus and Serena), and how unquestioning belief and the Law of Attraction led to the latter becoming two of the world's greatest ever tennis players. (This was something that most people in the privileged white tennis hierarchy considered completely impossible for teenage African-American girls who were born into a non-tennis playing family in the socioeconomically disadvantaged suburb of Compton.)

Thus, through theories of unity, interconnectedness, entanglement, superposition, and instant and long-term manifestations, it is possible to form a more scientific conceptualisation of 'oneness', and for motivated individuals to draw on such ideas in order to become more empowered and skilled at generating positive change in the world.

Other Evidence of a Living Universe

In *Synchronicity: The Bridge Between Matter and Mind,* F. David Peat provides a wealth of evidence to demonstrate that the universe itself is a living, intelligent, and participatory force. For example, Peat claims that the phenomenon of superconductivity arises from a form of cooperative and collective order. He notes that when vibrating atoms reach a critical temperature, they start to work in a cohesive rather than disruptive way, thereby allowing the efficient movement of electrical current. In other words, at a critical point, random electron motion no longer results in resistance, and an important transition occurs such that the entire system starts to act cooperatively as a whole at the quantum level (all oppositions to flow disappear).

Peat also sees evidence of a living, intelligent, and participatory universe in relation to the scientific processes of order returning after a period of non-linearity, disorder, and chaos. For instance, he states that once the power of a system is increased, it leaves the known linear region and enters the more complex, unfamiliar world of non-linear effects: turbulence, overload, distortion, deformation, explosions, uncontrollable oscillations, buckling, fracturing, and collapse can all result. What is of particular interest, however, is that non-linear effects are not ultimately completely destructive, but lead to the emergence of new forms of structure. Again, it is at critical points – that is, at the non-linear stage (or 'the straw that broke the camel's back') – that drastic effects or unexpected discontinuities occur. Peat claims that where chaos has set in due to competing flows, then the whole system will move from disorder into order when a certain critical point is reached. It is at this time that random movements will suddenly transform into large-scale flows and order will return, or emerge anew. Thus, while the universe may be in a constant state of flux (a perpetual unfolding), it is also characterised by deeper underlying patterns that make all things connected. Knowledge of such connectedness can greatly empower and enhance the skills of any individual seeking to create a better world on multiple levels.

As indicated previously, it is through such examples (and many other quantum theories) that Peat is able to explain how the universe is in fact alive and, therefore, humans are able to manifest synchronicities (that is, outer manifestations which mirror inner processes of mind). He argues that there are powerful symmetries (or inner patterns) in both nature and the psyche that can generate acausal parallelisms. These can be thought of as meaningful arrangements which reveal a universe that unfolds according to a hidden, dynamic order. Peat says that synchronistic thinking lies outside time and space, and it is a manifestation of a much wider principle of acausal orderedness (part of The Unified Field) which is also found in quantum theory.

Many-Worlds Theory (The Multiverse)

In 1956, Hugh Everett formulated the idea that all possibilities simultaneously occur in a multiverse comprised of independent parallel universes. It has been further postulated that there is some kind of mechanism for interaction between these universes, such that all states are accessible (and able to be impacted on). Physicists like Richard Feynman and Stephen Hawking have embraced this theory, and notions of there being Many Worlds or a Multiverse provide levels of empowerment for agents of global change that wider humanity is only just starting to conceive.

Consciousness Is All There Is

Some quantum theorists have also suggested that many key scientific discoveries (or findings or revelations) are now aligning with more spiritual conceptions of consciousness. David Albert's *Quantum Mechanics and Experience* is one text that explores this alignment from a philosophy of physics perspective. In accordance with The Observer Effect is the assertion that because particles act differently when they are being observed, then they are actually aware of when they are being watched (they can be anywhere when unobserved, but in a predictable location when watched). In this theory, there is a clear relationship between 'the observer' and 'the observed', and the former actively impacts on the latter. Alternatively, it may be that particles exist nowhere other than when they are being observed – in other words, it is only consciousness that creates the appearance of particles. According to key ideas advanced by a number of physicists in the television series *Through the Wormhole*, this ties in with the idea that it is only consciousness that creates reality [everything] and, as such, there is no separability. Thus, something may exist in multiple places and yet be in none of these places until somebody actually looks (that is, things do not come into existence until the act of observation occurs). Particles may, then, be merely momentary manifestations of an imaginary realm (pure consciousness). As is explained in the *Down the Rabbit Hole* documentary, there is no subject-object split in many spiritual understandings of enlightenment. Indeed, there is no 'I'-ness or separateness, and humans have only become 'two' (spirit and soul) for the sake of experience. As well, just as 'space' is an artificial construct, 'time' itself may only exist in consciousness.

Essentially, then, these theories suggest that while there is only unity, there may be the appearance of many manifestations (or many intelligences) within the one consciousness. Nonetheless, all in the universe is united waves of vibration, so, ultimately, everybody and everything is one. As such, an effective path to enlightenment may be experiencing unbounded consciousness (that is, coming to the knowledge that consciousness itself is infinite). For many agents of positive world change, the quantum-level concepts relating to Unity and Infinity are thus both highly inspiring and empowering.

*Readers should note that there are members of the scientific community who have significant issues with the New Age linking of quantum theory and consciousness. This book presents a very brief introduction to key concepts being explored at what some may regard as the 'fringe' of science. By investigating pioneering physicists and the major theories that led to the development of modern quantum mechanics, individuals can formulate their own opinions regarding the usefulness of quantum theory in bringing conceptions of consciousness to wider humanity and the resulting possibility of positive global transformation. Key physicists include Max Planck; Albert Einstein; Louis de Broglie; Edwin Schrodinger; Max Born; Werner Heisenberg; Niels Bohr; David Bohm; Richard Feynman; and Stephen Hawking.

[NB Please see Appendix B for a wider ranging survey of the universal nature of the Infinity concept – such universality imbuing it with the power to unify diverse peoples across the entire world (thereby working to create a preferable future for the whole of humanity).]

CHAPTER 7
EMPOWERING AGENTS OF POSITIVE WORLD CHANGE THROUGH VARIOUS FORMS OF GUIDANCE

When the universe is understood as a source of Infinite wisdom which humanity can access (or communicate with) at any time, then individuals can feel assured that they are never alone. Such knowledge ensures trust that when they are faced with difficult life challenges, a person can seek assistance or support from an unlimited, eternally available energy. By being truly open to accepting the support being sought – whether it is coming from some kind of quantum- or higher-level intelligence - then it will manifest (and deliver any other crucial information) in ways that are suited to each individual. Help can arrive in many shapes and forms: it may be a message sent from the unconscious (for example, as a dream or visual fantasy laden with symbols of great personal relevance); the central themes of a book, film, or artwork being interacted with; the positive attitude of a new co-worker or fellow workshop participant; or a series of signs and synchronicities that imbue trust and faith in the path being pursued and the knowledge that, ultimately, the most beneficial experiences are being provided for greater world improvement. Such awareness can enhance personal growth, as well as bring an increased sense of strength; empowerment; happiness; and hope. Invigorating mystical occurrences can thus provide invaluable guidance for those on the path to realising their wider life purpose. In honouring a deeper understanding of one's broader planetary role, it is then possible to work in ways that provide benefit to humanity and the environment at the macrocosmic level.

Myths, Archetypes, and The Collective Unconscious
In the course of developing their theories regarding mental health and the psyche, Sigmund Freud and Carl Gustav Jung (*Man and His Symbols*) drew heavily on myths, archetypes, and the notion that there is a collective unconscious which operates as a reservoir of universally shared ideas and symbols. Freud primarily focused on the myths of ancient cultures that he held as being instrumental in shaping the Western psyche. Most famously, he utilised the Greek

myth about Oedipus killing his father and marrying his mother to describe the Oedipal Complex, in which men play out certain life patterns as a result of being 'in love' with their mothers.

Jung extended this theory by investigating the myths of a wide variety of traditional Indigenous cultures from around the world, and by developing the idea that there are 'universally common' archetypes that the psyche either identifies with, or which it attracts into its life in order to play out certain archetypal stories. For instance, in the course of an individual's personal 'Hero's Journey' (their archetypal life story) they may play the role of seeker when young, thereby attracting an older teacher for an important period of learning or training during key years. As they grow in wisdom, they may then become a kind of messenger and subsequently attract supporters who fulfil a different archetypal function.

Major archetypes can also appear in an individual's life in a cyclical way until they have learnt (or 'figured out') how to resolve a recurring issue, drama, or trauma (possibly stemming from childhood or early adulthood). A man may, for example, play out complex psychological processes relating to his 'loss of boyhood' (innocence) and 'transition into manhood' (difficult knowledge) over the course of a lifetime by progressively mentoring young males at different ages (mid-teens, late-teens, early twenties) until he realises what patterns are occurring and how the fundamental associated lessons can be integrated into his psyche. For Jung, in particular, this kind of process can be a path to self-realisation (wholeness and completion).

As such, knowledge of wider archetypal stories and roles can enable individuals to understand why they must face and surmount certain life challenges (a kind of empowerment for achieving life purpose), as well as how their personal evolution is part of a much greater reality and agenda (that being the creation of a better world). Indeed, the entire notion of a collective unconscious would suggest that there are cosmic patterns playing out in the lives of many people across time (numerous generations and lifetimes) and space (in multiple languages and different geographical locations around the world). When psychics and tarot readers are doing large-scale presentations (such as in front of live audiences or via widely-accessed online videos), there is now increasingly a claim that the readings are relevant to everybody in the room (even if they seem to only be solicited from the guides of one individual), or to the entire collective / soul tribe that has been drawn to watching them.

Dreams, Fantasies, and Astral Travel

One of the most important reasons behind why it is essential to have adequate amounts of sleep each day, is that the unconscious mind is actively sending key symbols and messages in the form of dreams. Freud and Jung (*Memories, Dreams, Reflections*) were major pioneers in the use of dream, fantasy, and daydream interpretation and analysis during psychotherapy. Such psychodynamic approaches were employed as a way to advance the individuation process (realisation of the self), and thereby allow an individual to achieve psychological wholeness and the elimination of neuroses. Jung, in particular, would advocate the benefits of daily dream (and fantasy) recording and review as a way to psychologically integrate the deeper meaning of all events and relationships and, thus, enhance overall psychic growth as a fundamental component of realising one's greater life purpose. In this way, messages coming from dreams can be used as a form of personal empowerment in order to more effectively work at creating a better world.

Lucid dreaming can be another path to gaining memorable and useful messages. While most dreams are recalled only after waking, in the lucid state the individual is able to enter into a kind of light sleep and actively dream whilst remaining conscious of all that is unfolding. Many people have also claimed that they can actually control or direct what is occurring in their dreams whilst lucid, which may be a particularly useful step in preparing for more advanced forms of astral travel.

Through astral and celestial travel - which can occur unconsciously in the sleep state, or via a more deliberate (conscious) form of projection - it is possible to enter other planes and access knowledge and wisdom that can provide guidance on the journey to life purpose realisation. According to *The Lightworker's Guide to the Astral Realm* by Sahvanna Arienta, knowledge of the multiverse can be actively sought out by first setting a clear intention and raising one's vibrational level (such as by deliberately selecting positive thoughts). Arienta claims that the ultimate aim of astral and celestial travel is to expand consciousness and learn compassion for everyone; tolerance of difference; and an understanding of unity with all creation. She says that the intelligence of the universe is always available through astral and celestial journeys: it can be tapped into at any time, and by anyone who has progressively developed their energetic capacities (that is, by increasing their vibrations). As well, soul travel can enable individuals to go on journeys that will help them access invaluable information for healing personal trauma, coping with minor day-to-day difficulties, and solving big life problems. Visiting other realms can further allow humans to comprehend that there are more important things than the material trappings of the Earth plane. Such realisations can then result in people moving beyond irrational ego-based fears, and giving up items that they may have been hoarding (or unhealthy relationships they may have been maintaining) as a result of a 'loss' mentality. Enhanced forms of psychological liberation and emotional freedom can subsequently promote an individual's positivity and, thus, vibrational levels, which ensures that they are then able to access even more assistance from other realms (such that the path to personal wisdom and inner peace becomes a perpetual upward-spiralling loop).

A large number of people who have had out-of-body experiences – which, similarly, can occur with or without conscious direction - and near-death experiences (for instance, during the coma state) also report that they have been provided with great insight into what their soul is doing on the Earth plane, as well as lasting forms of enlightenment about how it all ties in to a greater level of reality. Books such as Dannion and Kathryn Brinkley's *Secrets of the Light*; Eben Alexander's *Proof of Heaven*; and Jim Willis' *Guide to Out-of-Body Experiences for the Astral Traveller* provide detailed accounts of several individuals connecting with the higher realms. In near-death experiences, patterns of seeing the light; meeting spirit guides or passed-over loved ones; and experiencing a life review have all been commonly documented prior to a person's entry into a 'state of bliss'. Willis also explores ways that an individual can connect to universal consciousness, which can then be a vital empowerment process for those who have a greater life purpose to achieve on Earth. He says that out-of-body experiences and near-death experiences can allow humans to realise that they are more than their physical bodies, and that entering into peaceful nothingness is in itself a form of liberation. This kind of awakening to the highest level of consciousness (or immaterial essence) by escaping one's bodily confines while fully conscious is a clear and direct way for people to understand how they can share their experiences in order to create a better reality for others on the Earth plane.

Signs and Symbols

In order to maximise higher levels of guidance and assistance whilst working to generate positive world change, it is essential that each individual develops their own tapestry of relevant signs and symbols, as well as an awareness that interpretations of these can change or evolve over the course of a lifetime. Signs and symbols can be very personal in nature, or they can have much wider cultural and universal significance. For instance, in line with their own particular life experiences, a divorced person may come to see a wedding ring as symbolising oppression (and, as such, a plain gold band will appear in their dreams whenever they are feeling trapped in real life), while a happily married person will regard a ring as a symbol of love. In Western culture, the ring commonly represents commitment, while from a more universal perspective it may signify the cycle of life.

Individuals can develop distinct or overlapping personal, cultural, and universal understandings of the significance or symbolism of everything that exists in the world. Both living things (flora and fauna) and inanimate objects (home items and public structures) can be interpreted in unique ways by different people (such as an eagle representing either predatory behaviours or freedom), or they can symbolise the same thing to large groups within a particular culture or belief system (like the cross meaning sacrifice and salvation for Christians). Everything from colours to numbers can be understood in symbolic terms. For instance, red can convey anger or passion, and 222 can signify partnership.

Doreen Virtue's *Signs From Above* provides a good introduction to the shared meaning of a wide range of signs and symbols. Listed below are some of the signs or symbols which are interpreted in common ways by many people, and which can be used as forms of messages, guidance, and empowerment that assist with the creation of a preferable world.

- Finding a coin on the footpath can be regarded as a sign that change or good fortune is imminent, or, alternatively, that an individual is 'on the money' with respect to what they are thinking about at the time of discovery.

- A butterfly can signify that an individual is about to experience a big life transformation.
- A spider's web can be understood as a symbol for the interconnectedness of all life.
- Feathers can be interpreted as a sign that angels are nearby and providing assistance.
- A key can be regarded as a solution for a life problem or issue, or as something that can 'open new doors' (finding a key on the ground may mean that a resolution or new opportunity is coming).

It is important to remember that guidance can come in any form, from any source, and at any time. By staying alert and consciously interacting with all cultural forms (rather than simply using popular culture artefacts as a way to 'switch off' and escape reality), it is possible to discover a myriad of relevant messages and ideas that are frequently being sent. Being aware of, noting, and giving thanks for any helpful signs and symbols that appear in daily life can encourage an increased appearance of them, and can deepen a connection to other forms of guidance. When dealing with major life challenges, it is also crucial to look for (and follow) repetitive signs – their magnitude and consistency are key to how transformational the level of assistance being offered may be. According to Doreen Virtue, if there is ever any difficulty in interpreting them, it is possible to specifically ask one's guides for different signs that are more obvious or personally relevant and comprehensible. Ultimately, all signs have a specific purpose: to provide a sense of comfort or confirmation; to help with decision-making in the pursuit of important goals; or to support the following of certain life paths. Openness, receptivity, and a willingness to value and heed signs is, then, a sure way to invite their proliferation and trust the help being provided in the pursuit of creating a better world.

Guides

In *Contact Your Spirit Guides to Enrich Your Life,* Cassandra Eason presents the notion that guides are manifestations of an individual's higher self, and that they act (or present information) in external ways which make each person feel comfortable. For instance, mediums may feel supported when they see apparitions of deceased loved ones, while psychotherapists steeped in Freudian theory may feel more at ease receiving guidance from famous or known figures who appear in their dreams (each person embodying a symbolically relevant archetype for the dreamer). Ultimately, whether it is from the most evolved part of the human soul, or some higher energy force, it is possible for individuals to access universal wisdom and insight from all times and places. Invisible friends, guardian angels, enlightened sages, and other kinds of guides aim to provide help and improve people's lives – they are infinitely wise and not constrained by physical time or space.

In *Wisdom From Your Spirit Guides,* James Van Praagh claims that guides can send specific signs to help individuals cope with difficult situations and overcome obstacles, or to provide assurance that healthy decisions are being made. Guides are, however, constrained by an individual's free will, meaning that they can only provide assistance when requested (consciously or unconsciously), and can only continue with aid when a person is truly open to receiving and following guidance. If an individual decides to override the messages of help, the guides will withdraw and allow them to pursue their own path (this can often lead to acts of self-sabotage until a person is prepared to trust in direction from their higher self). Guides are particularly active when they are assisting people who are committed to working on their own healing, or who are trying to create a better world by promoting wider evolution for all of humanity.

Van Praagh identifies several guides that an individual may have, including:

- The Master Guide – often the most dominant guide who acts like a teacher or mentor for the duration of a person's life (they may use specific or characteristic signs and symbols to indicate their presence and convey important messages);
- Inspiration Guide – this guide encourages individuals to be true to themselves by presenting clues for how to move beyond ego, follow the heart, and channel inspirational ideas for creations that will help transform the world's consciousness;
- Relationship Guide – the primary focus of this guide is the personal growth that can occur through experiences of love (including learning to open one's heart to the right karmically-connected person, acquiring strategies to cope with relationship difficulties, and developing the self-worth needed to attract healthy forms of love); and

- Protector Guides – these guides actively work to keep people away from lower-level energies, sending clear signs (which can manifest as physical responses) when an individual should move away from a toxic or harmful person, or remove themselves from a negative or dangerous situation.

Van Praagh also outlines ways in which an individual can work most effectively with their guides. He provides some of the following tips:

1. Focus on integrity and a higher life purpose to attract the interest and support of the guides.
2. Raise and sustain personal energy levels (in the form of both vibrations and luminosity) to transmit and receive thoughts, feelings, and images.
3. Maintain a sense of positivity so that the guides feel welcome / invited to make contact and communicate. This can be done by embracing enthusiasm, inner power, and wisdom, as well as projecting an energy of love. Breathing in joy and exhaling stress and negative thinking can further promote connection (as can letting go of confusion and limited beliefs).
4. Encourage the guides' presence by creating a space for them to enter. Grounding exercises can be utilised to establish a link between Earth and cosmic energies. Chakra points can also be unblocked to facilitate the guides (the crown chakra is regarded as a doorway to The Infinite).
5. Develop a conscious relationship with individual guides.
6. Frequently ask the guides if they have any relevant information to pass on, or a particular mission with which they need assistance.
7. Be open-minded and pay close attention to all signs and symbols, plus any associated visions, thoughts, mental impressions, emotions, or physical responses. Be sure to then apply and live the guidance that is delivered.
8. Show gratitude for all forms of awareness, insight, and knowledge. This can be done by giving a sincere form of thanks for wherever the information received may lead.

For those who feel comfortable with such ideas, guides may be a useful way to access important information that will assist with the creation of a better world.

Imaginal Guides

In *The Practice of Ally Work,* Jeffrey Raff explains that the worlds of myth and fiction (whether expressed through literary, musical, artistic, or screen culture) are rich in imaginal characters who are able to provide specific forms of inspiration and guidance. For example, the 'pot of gold at the end of the rainbow' is regarded by many as a symbol of not just personal attainment and happiness, but actually complete spiritual fulfilment. The leprechaun holding this pot of gold can, then, be seen as the imaginal guide who is able to lead an individual to awakening and greater awareness. For an individual who is pursuing a spiritual path, all cultural references to (or image-based appearances of) the leprechaun may work as reinforcement that they are on the right path, or that their efforts are being overseen by a higher energy.

There is no shortage of mythic and fictional characters who can be regarded as guides at different phases of the life journey. For generations heavily steeped in the D.C., Harry Potter, or Marvel imaginal worlds, there are endless heroic types to draw on for symbolic affinity (from the ingenuity of Batman to the strength of Thor). A television show like *Dexter* also follows the existential journey of a character who interacts with many individuals fulfilling key Freudian roles or Jungian archetypes (including the sibling, soul mate, best friend, mentor, and protégé) whilst exploring what it means to be human and to ultimately understand what love truly is. For those suffering from existential angst, Dexter Morgan may prove to be a suitable imaginal guide because he is often coming to terms with (or learning about) issues of morality at the most fundamental level – a years-long process that works as a kind of evolving healing after deep childhood trauma. Whatever the particular needs of an individual's psyche or general life circumstances at any given time, there is no doubt that an imaginal figure can appear to provide the most appropriate forms of guidance whenever a genuine request is made (either consciously or unconsciously) for personal empowerment and the assistance required on the path to creating a better world.

Nature Guides and Power Animals

James Van Praagh (*Wisdom From Your Spirit Guides*) notes that nature guides can take the form of natural elements (such as flowers, trees, mountains, rivers, oceans, lightning, the wind); actual creatures (like birds, animals, insects, and sea life); or protectors that may be invisible to most (fairies and gnomes). Many people regard their pets as being guardian angels sent to comfort, heal, or protect them at key junctures in the course of their life. Pets can show their owners unconditional love - as well as activate it within them - and they can provide enormous care during a person's greatest time of need.

In the book *Shamanism,* Will Adcock also documents the concept of a power animal, which is an ally that can be called on to provide insight and guidance at any time. Different animals embody key characteristics (both strengths and weaknesses). A person's country of origin and cultural background can heavily influence the range of natural and human associations that they have with specific regional native animals. In an increasingly globalised world, individuals may additionally feel comfortable identifying with power animals which have symbolic significance in other geographic locations. For instance, an Australian person may feel an affinity with the quiet, reclusive nature of the platypus, but they may be equally influenced by Native American worldviews, and so ultimately identify the moose (a symbol of strength and wisdom) as their true power animal.

Many individuals from traditional Indigenous backgrounds have deep personal relationships with their totem animal/s according to their particular role in a kinship clan. Westerners are, however, more inclined to embrace the dominant qualities of their domestic pets. The enormous variety of dog and cat breeds (as well as fish, reptiles, rabbits, and guinea pigs) means that there is a wide range of traits that individuals can come to embody from a power animal perspective (such as the 'hard working' mentality of dogs like blue heelers and kelpies). People from farming backgrounds often have a strong connection to the animals that they are interacting with on a daily basis as well. For example, Asian peoples who work with oxen may value slower, contemplative behaviours, while Mediterranean peoples who herd goats may appreciate the virtue of determination. In searching for an appropriate power animal who will bring guidance, an individual can consider what different animals symbolise, then select one which has the qualities they most wish to incorporate into their life whilst working to create a better world.

Shamanic Journeys

In the aforementioned book *Shamanism,* Will Adcock explains that many cultures regard spirit as being an omnipresent energy (imbued in all things), as well as the essence of creation and the unifying force present throughout the entire universe. A large number of Indigenous peoples (from Asia, Austronesia, Africa, and the Americas) believe that this energy extends beyond the physical realm, and so can be accessed for purposes of guidance, healing, and wisdom. Many traditional cultures continue to rely on a shaman who is able to raise their energy vibrations such that they can communicate with other parts of the natural world, and thereby act as an intermediary between the people and spirits of the earth (delivering messages from a higher realm). Adcock argues that for Indigenous peoples, deeply connecting with nature is about appreciating it; showing gratitude to the earth and its creatures; and learning humility whilst carrying out duties and responsibilities in the care of the land and wildlife over the course of a lifetime.

Adcock also claims that shamanic journeys can be healing, inspirational, or empowering, and can involve the use of a power object from nature (for instance, a stone or a feather), or a power symbol (such as a word, picture, or song relevant to the natural world). He says that shamans set clear intentions prior to embarking on a journey: they state specific reasons for going; request any required help; and remain open to support coming in unexpected ways. Shamanic journeys can lead 'downwards' (into caves or bodies of water like wells, rivers, and oceans) in the seeking of solutions and greater spiritual understanding. On such journeys, a series of challenges may be encountered (as a symbolic form of confronting and overcoming individual or societal problems and fears) so that the conscious self can resolve any matters of concern. Surmounting obstacles and opponents with creativity and logic is an important empowerment process for devising ways around or through a difficult issue. By dealing with, and getting beyond, anything that is blocking passage, there comes a knowledge of how to exert control over others and self. Shamanic journeys can also be taken 'upwards' (to the place of the higher self) for purposes of inspiration and communion with other spirits. Visits to the 'underworld' are about dealing with what lies within, while the 'upperworld' is a light and limitless space where it is possible to elicit assistance from others. 'Underworld' journeys are important for learning *how* to complete projects aimed at creating a better reality for humanity and the environment, while the 'upperworld' notion of limitlessness is extremely empowering for individuals exploring multiple possibilities in how to transform the world.

Earth Guides

Earth guides are everyday people such as neighbours, relatives, friends, or even strangers who seemingly appear out of nowhere to in some way assist an individual on their path. One theory is that everybody who appears in an individual's life is part of their soul family. Soul families are groups of souls (human and animal) who travel through different lifetimes together, and who occupy distinct roles according to the lessons to be learned in each incarnation. For instance, in one life a particular soul may play the 'villain', and in subsequent lives they may embody the role of the 'hero'. In other words, different members of the group fulfil different 'contracts' with each other in each lifetime. Soul contracts are pacts made between souls (before their physical incarnations) to help each other in some way. It is important to remember that even those individuals who are appearing to engage in 'negative' behaviours may be crucial for a soul's ultimate psychic development. Indeed, it is often the problematic actions of others that provide the most significant catalysts for resolving fundamental life traumas and recurring personal issues, as well as for learning important lessons and achieving greater purposes like generating positive change in the world.

According to James Van Praagh (*The Power of Love*), soul family members can either engage in seriously challenging behaviours, or they can provide more harmonious forms of assistance in the shape of advice, insights, and support. Either way, they can have an invaluable impact on how an individual's life subsequently plays out (in accordance with each predetermined soul contract created prior to incarnation). People - and the life events experienced with them - are 'tools' from which an individual can learn. Soul lessons are not always easy, but they are an essential part of a greater plan for spiritual growth and healing or fixing a 'broken' world. When facing obstacles or difficult times, it is possible to ask for the appearance of a real-life connection who can provide recognition of one's strengths and greatest potential, as well as practical comfort and suggested coping strategies. This person will also undoubtedly be deeply honest and foreground integrity and encouragement to remain on the path to creating a preferable future for the planet.

Given that humans are able to receive guidance regarding every aspect of their lives, it is important for individuals to appreciate and give thanks for each occurrence that leads to greater knowledge and awareness. The more rapidly an individual can reinterpret what may at first appear to be 'bad', the more easily they can enjoy the benefits of hindsight and recognise that certain 'failures' or 'tragedies' may have actually been an important doorway to great advancement for themselves and the world as a whole.

Anam Caras and Soul Mates

The Irish recognise an 'anam cara' as a soul friend – somebody who is crucial to an individual's life journey, and who may appear at a key turning point in order to fundamentally alter a person's life so that they go on to achieve their greater life purpose. According to *Anam Cara* by John O'Donohue, this soul friend can be a mentor, lover, spiritual guide, or somebody else of significance. Meeting an anam cara can inspire an individual to drop all their external facades and internal delusions. Showing the true self and sharing one's innermost mind can subsequently create transformative circumstances that lead to an awakening (this can include the individual's role in working to transform the world for the better). There is a deep soul-level love at play in all interactions with an anam cara. By entering into a complete state of trust with them, an individual can be prompted to take important life action; deepen their personal knowledge; or be guided to a higher realisation of how they can define who they truly are, and thereby fulfil their ultimate agenda on the planet.

According to Tanya Carroll Richardson (*MindBodyGreen*), a soul mate is, similarly, somebody with whom an individual has some kind of special connection. In the physical realm this may manifest as aligned values and beliefs; a commitment to common goals; or shared life themes. While soul mates may be romantic partners (as the phrase is often understood in popular culture contexts), they can also be relatives, friends, colleagues, or even animals with whom there is deep compatibility. It is possible to have multiple soul mates - either simultaneously or progressively - throughout the course of life. These important supports can serve a range of different purposes, and may appear intermittently, for a short period of time, or consistently over the course of many years. A soul mate is often someone who can be communicated with in an open and intimate way; a person who provides assistance during difficult life events; or an individual who brings much-needed inspiration and motivation at crucial times – such as when a major world-changing project is being worked on. As well, soul mates can be mirrors, providing a reflection of personal strengths (best qualities) and weaknesses (insecurities and flaws). They are most helpful when being completely honest and working as either a mentor or catalyst (deliberately or inadvertently) via shared journey interactions.

Many people have a feeling of familiarity or 'clicking' when they meet a soul mate. This sense of automatic resonance may be due to soul mates vibrating at a similar frequency, or because of a predetermined plan (made prior to incarnation) to connect at a key point in life. As such, soul mates can know each other intimately, and therefore provide the right kind of assistance during periods of dedication to a higher cause like bringing positive change to the world. They also have unconditional love for each other at the highest level, and so are able to offer profound (overt or subtle) life guidance. By letting go of superficial behaviours (including substance abuse, jealousy, materialism, and greed), an individual is more likely to attract the right kind of practical support at major stages of the life journey. Identifying and committing to a greater life purpose can further invite genuinely compatible human connections. Ultimately, soul mates appear to assist with processes of personal evolution (such as ego dissolution), and a person's further movement into states of trust, self-awareness (self-knowledge), receptivity, and non-judgement (including greater forms of love, understanding, and acceptance for self and others). A soul mate's contribution, then, can be extremely valuable in terms of the extensive input they provide in assisting a person to engage in transformative global actions of a positive nature.

Old souls can also be deeply sensitive, highly empathetic, and emotionally aware individuals who are committed to notions of compassion, love, and peace. There are many old souls who are actively involved in making a difference or improving the world at a macrocosmic level. Since they are usually very stable, rational, and calm in their approach to life, they can be extremely important connections. Indeed, individuals can greatly benefit from drawing on an old soul's intuitive and revelatory insights regarding life purpose fulfilment, and how to survive major challenges whilst working to create a better world.

Twin Souls

Twin souls are individuals who are not related by blood, but who have had phenomenally similar life experiences. They may also have had some uncanny indicators (throughout the course of their lives, but prior to actually meeting) that their 'twin' is out there. Twin souls will undoubtedly have shared communication styles, interests, values, beliefs, and life agendas. They may have been brought up in very similar ways, but on different sides of a country or continent. As well, they have probably been through some virtually identical life processes – such as being exposed to the same kinds of early cultural influences; surviving parallel relationship breakdowns; or enduring the same forms of hardship (like incarceration for a common justice cause). It may be that one of the twins is slightly older than the other, in which case they can recognise exactly what the younger twin is going through and provide them with invaluable guidance as the latter journeys through common life events. As with biological twins, spiritually connected twin souls can often feel, or know exactly, what the other person is experiencing. The communication between twin souls can be telepathic in nature (leading to an innate form of knowing), or one person may be inundated with cultural references, synchronicities, and other kinds of external stimuli that make them fully aware of what their twin is dealing with. Twin souls may also have complementary skills or abilities such that, when they come together to work as a team, they form a complete partnership that can allow them to make major advancements and actively change the world in profoundly beneficial ways.

Twin Flames

According to several articles by Aletheia Luna and Mateo Sol (*LonerWolf*), twin flames are partners who will catalyse spiritual maturing and conscious expansion; assist each other with fulfilling true life mission; and aid the planet's collective growth towards harmony. These souls feel connected physically, emotionally, intellectually, spiritually, karmically, and cosmically, as they may have agreed to reincarnate together across multiple (or all) lifetimes. As such, twin flames may feel completely overwhelmed when they first meet, as they might have significant existential issues to resolve before being willing and able to work together on a shared higher cause. There may also be a protracted period of ego deconstruction and major life change before a couple can successfully collaborate. In addition, one of the twins may have to push the other to confront their insecurities and fears (or transcend the ego state) before they feel capable of operating as equals on an important world improvement task.

When twin flames meet, Luna and Sol claim that they may feel:
- an instant recognition (such as via déjà vu, destiny, inevitability, a past life connection, or an intense sense of 'home');
- a resonance on the deepest spiritual level and a need to unite (due to two eternal obligations coming together);
- an awareness of being finely tuned to each other's energies (including an ability to communicate telepathically);
- a deep soul connection (such as through shared values, beliefs, and goals), and a sense of having a greater agenda with each other (like working on a joint project to create a better world);
- a feeling of expansion (including that time does not actually exist; knowing that all external facades are transparent; and an understanding that honesty and authenticity are always possible since unconditional love and mutual forgiveness are able to trump fear of rejection, persecution, and judgement);
- a 'magnetic' attraction related to what is most desired for inner healing and world improvement (and often, simultaneously, a 'repelling' due to a fundamental fear of becoming psychically whole); and
- a multi-level connectedness (as friends; lovers; guides for personal growth and transformation; mentors to becoming the best possible versions of self; and partners who need to complete a higher purpose of wider social or ecological benefit).

The Future of Love

Daphne Rose Kingma's revelatory book *The Future of Love* also provides deep insight into how higher purpose relationships are set to become increasingly important in coming years. Kingma argues that relationships in gatherer-hunter and agricultural societies were largely formed as a result of survival needs, with males and females fulfilling key roles (according to gender-based traditions or their biological sex attributes). She then claims that much of humanity entered into (and is largely still in) a period of 'personality' or 'ego-based' relationships. This era has been defined by people trying to use romantic relationships as a way to get all their emotional, psychological, and physical needs met – often in a selfish way, and thereby giving rise to partners engaging in competitive behaviours that lead to conflict or unsatisfactory forms of compromise. Breeding to perpetuate the species or family name have been common in both these types of pairings.

Kingma says that increasingly (now and in the future), relationships will revolve around two people coming together to fulfil a higher cause, and, as a result of this, they will experience a very deep form of love. Couples will find a great sense of personal fulfilment and happiness in such unions due to the fact that both partners will be committed to transcending ego (and petty personal desires) so that they can remain aligned in realising their larger life purpose (that is, in conjunction). As such, trivial arguments and rivalries will be replaced by individuals willingly making sacrifices in order to stay united – this will then enable them to use their combined skills to achieve a greater good for the wider benefit of humanity and the environment. In these kinds of relationships, mutual consciousness and cooperation are key to the resolution of all intimate and wider social problems. In order to achieve their greater purpose, karmically aligned couples may find that they have complementary skill sets, and may also frequently access and receive large amounts of higher-level guidance in order to create a better world together.

Lightworkers, Spiritual Messengers, and Cosmic Messengers

Lightworkers are people who bring a spiritual dimension to their actions. They are aligned to the highest plan for Earth, and will work consciously to channel light (love) while assisting humanity to realise it. This mission requires lightworkers to attain increased levels of compassion, care, and consideration for all living things; to understand the equality of everything; and to work in harmony with natural cycles. Lightworkers can operate in any field: they may be healers, teachers, film directors, political lobbyists, volunteer charity workers, or full-time mothers. Since its inception, the Australian Indigenous Dance Company Bangarra has been populated with choreographers, dancers, and musicians who are undoubtedly operating as lightworkers. Bangarra has consistently produced spiritually rich performances that are not only visually breathtaking, but which have the higher purpose agenda of revitalising traditional Aboriginal and Torres Strait Islander knowledges, and bringing greater public awareness to a wide range of contemporary social and political issues of pressing concern. (The documentary *Firestarter* is a moving tribute to the deeply soulful natures of Bangarra's founding Page brothers.)

Spiritual messengers are also individuals who bring higher-plane information to broader humanity through any means and at any time. Their messages do not stem from any kind of judgemental dogma associated with institutionalised religions, but focus instead on notions of tolerance and oneness. [While some organised religions rely on hierarchical forms of power and wealth to aggressively spread beliefs that inspire guilt, fear, and discriminatory attitudes, most New Age approaches use kindness, compassion, and support as the basis for exploring spiritual ideas via workshops, books, and personal readings.] Spiritual messengers can appear in any form and frequently provide the reassuring message that no one is alone on their life journey - no matter how many serious difficulties or challenges a person may face in their time on planet Earth, they are always loved by a greater spiritual force.

According to Australian author Elizabeth Peru, cosmic messengers are people who work to bring humanity highly significant messages from the broader cosmos. During periods of astral or celestial travel, they may receive key ideas that they are required to share with the world. Important information may also be delivered to them via means such as ear transmissions (these are signified by a brief high-pitched sound in either ear, according to the nature of the material). Peru claims that such messengers have 'cosmic consciousness' through aligning their energy with the planets and stars (she describes energy, in general, as a 'moving wave of desire' coming from the cosmos).

By taking guidance from (or actually becoming) a lightworker, spiritual messenger, or cosmic messenger, then, an individual's life purpose is accelerated, and an increased number of synchronicities will manifest to guide them in the realisation of their higher cause (that being related to the creation of a preferable world reality for all of humanity).

CHAPTER 8
EMPOWERING AGENTS OF POSITIVE WORLD CHANGE THROUGH VARIOUS FORMS OF INSIGHT

Intuition

Intuition is often referred to as a 'gut feeling' or 'hunch', and is a perception of facts, truths, knowledge, or insight that is gained without relying on rational thought. Through using intuition, individuals can access all kinds of higher-level guidance, including who to trust, or who to form relationships with in order to experience important soul journeys that lead to greater wisdom. According to Shakti Gawain (*Developing Intuition*), intuition can come in the form of:
- strong feelings;
- a spontaneous insight;
- clear visions;
- a sense of knowing something without knowing why;
- the reception of specific information or key messages; and
- an overwhelming sense about a person or situation.

Developing intuitive skills can also help to attract more spiritually fulfilling personal circumstances. Gawain notes that intuition helps individuals to:
- make good decisions and positive choices;
- effectively deal with daily challenges;
- build self-trust and confidence;
- follow inner wisdom;
- understand what needs to be done to achieve life purpose; and
- be connected to one's essential spiritual nature and the soul level of existence.

With growing awareness, then, proponents of significant world change can regularly access increased levels of assistance via personal forms of intuition.

Ways to Develop Skills of Intuition

Intuition is a widely written (and published) about topic, and there are a large number of highly detailed and insightful books available on ways to develop intuitive skills. Cate Howell's *Intuition,* Angela Martin's *Practical Intuition,* and Philip Goldberg's *The Intuitive Edge* all provide a range of strategies that individuals can

adopt in order to enhance their powers of intuition. Some of their suggestions are listed below.
1. Believe that unconscious perception is possible.
2. Let go of repetitive thoughts and negative emotions that interfere with self-guidance and personal wisdom.
3. Move beyond past problems and contemporary worries in order to stay open to all aspects of the life experience.
4. Work to actively relieve anxiety, stress, fatigue, depression, physical illness, and any other blocks to intuitive awareness.
5. Choose a slower pace of life.
6. Give up toxic substances (drugs and alcohol), eat healthily, and take the time to do soulful forms of exercise.
7. Declutter personal environments so as to become more energised.
8. Ensure adequate amounts of quality sleep in order to access insights from dreams.
9. Pursue frequent self-reflection (such as through journal writing).
10. Broaden the mind (by travelling, reading widely, or taking higher educational opportunities).
11. Practise gratitude, forgiveness, and unconditional love.
12. Embrace joy and a sense of peace and well-being on a daily basis.
13. Maintain positive thinking, flexibility, and optimism when faced with difficult and challenging situations.
14. Use mental relaxation and meditation to activate higher levels of knowledge.
15. Pay purposeful and non-judgemental attention to the present.
16. Develop mindfulness (awareness, attention, and memory).
17. Regularly engage in acts of compassion and empathy (become cognisant of, and try to fully understand, other people's thoughts and feelings).
18. Give up limited expectations so as to more spontaneously respond to events as they unfold.
19. Develop an holistic worldview and see everything as significant and purposeful.
20. Recognise the greater meaning behind symbols, metaphors, and patterns.
21. Follow big life passions and value play and creativity as part of this.
22. Find balance in all life pursuits (body, mind, and soul).

Activities for Accessing Intuitive Information

In *Intuition: Unlock the Power!*, Cate Howell also outlines a variety of activities that individuals can engage in when working to elicit information from intuitive means. A brief summary of key approaches is provided below.

a) Ask, 'What do I need to be aware of?' or 'What do I need to know right now?' Observe the thoughts, feelings, and / or images that appear. Be receptive, accepting, and grateful for all that comes through. Acknowledge that some responses may be delayed. For example, a message may come at a later time in the form of a passage in a book; the central themes of a film; or a conversation with a respected elder. Key ideas and inspiration can often come to mind during periods of deep relaxation.

b) Write specific questions at the top of a page, then ask intuition for guidance and enter into 'automatic writing' mode to record the responses (let the answers flow). Writing can invite reflective processes, heightened awareness, and deep connection. One strategy is to write down the questions with the dominant hand, then answer by using the non-dominant hand (this allows access to the intuitive and creative part of the mind). It is important to then trust the information that appears on the paper.

c) Clear out old thoughts (fears, doubts, and confusion). Focus by centring. Ground to the earth. Feel a sense of expansion. Use the image of a ball of light to rise energy up through the body. Make note of all intuitive insights as they emerge.

d) Ask the mind for guidance when making important decisions by using 'yes' or 'no' questions during meditation. Note the physical response for each answer. For example, there may be a sense of great joy and relief in relation to 'yes' (or a feeling of being strongly drawn towards it). Alternatively, when 'no' is presented, there could be an experience of shutting down, numbness, or an intense kind of dread.

e) For more complex forms of decision making (when multiple possibilities are being considered), visualise going down different paths that are branching off in a range of directions. When travelling down each path, consider whether it feels comfortable; exceedingly difficult; or perhaps full of worthwhile challenges and surmountable obstacles (ultimately leading to a good place or the right destination). Use intuitive revelations to select the best path for psychic growth and fulfilment of life purpose.

Regardless of what strategies and activities are favoured for developing intuitive skills and accessing intuition, it is clear that there is a plethora of ways to connect to useful insights that may be fundamental for the creation of a better world.

Telepathy and Remote Viewing

Telepathy is the ability to send information *to* another person, or to receive information (words, symbols, images) *from* another person, without verbal communication, and regardless of how much distance may exist between the parties. Through clear thoughts, it is possible for individuals (or multiple people) to exchange important messages. Similarly, according to Laura Day in her deeply insightful book *How to Rule the World From Your Couch*, highly focused minds can also be responsible for the manifestation of specific outcomes in the physical world. For instance, Day argues that telepathy can be used to achieve such external results as:

- guiding or modifying the thoughts and behaviours of others;
- soliciting and attracting what is most beneficial for the world;
- redirecting the manipulative intentions of lower-level energies;
- gaining awareness of the most powerful and productive life paths to follow;
- knowing how to easily deal with challenging people and situations; and
- sending clear and effective directives to friends, family members, colleagues, and associates so as to create harmonious relationships.

One theory is that telepathic communication is always occurring between people, but individuals are not always consciously aware (or choose not to be actively cognisant) of every thought that is being transferred. Another common idea is that regular and very clear telepathic communication will occur between people who are deeply connected, and who have an important shared life agenda or greater purpose to achieve on the planet together.

While telepathy is about a transfer of information or energy between people, remote viewing is related more to perceiving (or perhaps even mentally visiting) locations that are physically and /

or temporally distant. Indeed, it may be possible to remotely view places that are not just spatially distant, but which exist in different times (past or future). Other humans may or may not be present in these locations, as the goal of remote viewing may not be to listen in on other people's conversations, but to observe and gather crucial knowledge about geographically significant spots (or to collect data from the objects contained within certain rooms). By employing skills like telepathic communication and remote viewing, an individual can therefore experience a greater connection to the diverse ways in which it is possible to gain knowledge, guidance, insight, and wisdom for improving the world.

Psychic Awareness and Mediumship

While a medium is an individual who can deliver messages from 'the other side' (for instance, from an individual's deceased friends or family members), a psychic is someone who can gain knowledge about a living person's past, present, and / or future (such as by communicating with their own, or the subject's, spirit guides). Some people can operate as *both* psychics and mediums, and many psychics can access information through a variety of means (though they may have a greater preference for one method of receiving messages). There are a wide range of contemporary books identifying the diverse ways in which psychic abilities operate, including Theresa Cheung's *Working With Your Sixth Sense*, Char Margolis' *Discover Your Inner Wisdom*, and Julie Soskin's *Are You Psychic?* According to these authors, psychic information can be received by 'tuning in' and practising mindfulness. As well, spirit communication can happen, or psychic information can be accessed, when the rational mind 'gets out of the way'.

Psychic insight can commonly be received through such methods as:
- clairvoyance (clear seeing) – the power to see something (such as mental images, inner visions, symbols, dreams, objects, places, colours, spirits, people, animals, or events) in the past, present, or future by using one's 'inner eyes' (internal visual insights);
- clairaudience (clear hearing) – gaining psychic impressions through sound and sensitive listening (including hearing voices, specific words, noises, auditory messages and warnings, songs and / or lyrics, and the sounds of nature);

- clairsentience (clear feeling, knowing, or thinking) – the ability to cognitively know by receiving insights through empathetic means (this can involve sensing the atmosphere in a room, reading the moods or auras of others, having physical responses like 'gut reactions' when things feel 'right' or 'wrong', and being able to sense people's emotions);
- clairalience (clear smelling) and clairambience (clear tasting) – coming to psychic knowledge through smells and tastes (such as of flowers, cigarettes, or food); and
- precognition (prior knowing) - the cognitive ability to predict outcomes before they occur.

Mediums and psychics may also use a variety of means to connect with an individual's deceased loved ones or spirit guides, or to otherwise come to knowledge of important messages to pass on. Some of these means include:
- psychometry – tuning in to the vibrational energy of an object (like a piece of jewellery or clothing frequently worn by somebody);
- reading a person's palm, face, aura, or body language;
- reading physical objects like tarot cards (an individual's psychic energy is projected onto a deck, then selections of relevant cards are made in an unconscious way);
- reading natural objects like runes, crystals, tea leaves, or shells; and
- identifying the deeper meanings behind a client's artwork or mandalas (their images and patterns being a reflection of the unconscious mind).

Tarot cards have become increasingly popular and diversified in recent times, with a wide range of themed decks being available from New Age stores, and public / group or private / individual tarot readings being regularly provided online. For those who are interested, there are multiple daily postings on YouTube and the official advice is to watch those videos that have the greatest energetic resonance for the viewer. *Turning Tides Tarot* is a particularly insightful example that frequently focuses on issues of justice and how the individual can become empowered and increasingly influential in their life purpose work. *White Feather Tarot* also deals with a range of common concerns faced by humanity, such as processes of change, the power of the subconscious mind, and the value of universal signs.

For anybody receiving psychic information, Bruce Way's *How to Interpret a Psychic Reading* is an invaluable resource. It is particularly important to remember that the guidance being delivered may not make sense for several days, weeks, months, or years (in Earth time), as there is actually no such thing as time in the spirit world. Receiving, and working with, psychic insights is thus an excellent way to gain a greater understanding of the 'non-existence' of space and time, and an ultimate sense of limitlessness (including the ability to always access all forms of knowledge for the creation of a better world).

Becoming Open to Receiving Psychic Information

In the book *Infinite Quest*, world-renowned psychic John Edward argues that people can develop psychic abilities through a range of different methods, thus each individual should stay open-minded and trust their inner voice regarding the most effective approaches to favour. He outlines a number of key strategies that can be employed to increase psychic capacities, and a selection of these is listed below.

1. It is important to work in conjunction with the universal energy (energetic force) that is within, and surrounding, everyone and everything.
2. Everybody has a higher-level support team that can be connected to for guidance at any time. By having trust and faith in the presence of guides; actively listening to them; and developing gratitude, appreciation, and respect for their protection and inspiration, it is possible to access insight whenever it is needed.
3. While it is important to have a certain level of confidence, it is more desirable to move beyond the ego state and to instead become a humble vessel via which messages can be delivered (that is, to simply allow the information to be received).
4. Ask specific questions to elicit clear answers and pose follow-up queries if greater insight is required.
5. Let go of negativity and raise personal vibrations through positive thinking and kind actions. Become a willing force for the universe to use.

Ultimately, people with highly developed psychic abilities are also able to gain deeper insight into what actions may be best to take when working to generate a more sustainable, equitable, peaceful, and healthier global society.

The Akashic Field and The Akashic Records

The Akashic Records have been described in a variety of ways by writers from a range of disciplines. While they are sometimes visualised as actual written records contained in large 'volumes' that are stored in a kind of astral library, Sandra Anne Taylor describes them as a 'vibrating storehouse' of information. In her comprehensive book *The Akashic Records*, she claims that they constitute consciousness (the energy of eternity), and that they can be accessed by anybody, anywhere, and at any time, because they are held in the ethers of the universe and vibrate all around and within humanity. She explains that the first element in creation was 'akasha' (space) and, as such, it exists in everything.

One understanding of The Akashic Records is that they are a constantly evolving record of past, present, and future thoughts and events (or even the whole spectrum of *all* possible futures). As such, they may act as a kind of 'universal memory' which provides relevant information about past life themes and issues whenever current life blockages are being faced (the notion of reincarnation, or multiple lives, continuing to be the cornerstone of innumerable spiritual beliefs around the world). Consulting The Akashic Records can also be an empowering process when working to create a better world, as they may provide invaluable guidance on how to best engage in acts of healing and problem solving whenever an individual is struggling to cope with challenging times. Thus, Taylor claims that The Akashic Records can be regarded as both esoteric (embodying all the mysteries of life) and very practical (containing material that is relevant to every endeavour). This means they can be utilised by any individual who is seeking daily wisdom, and who may be receptive to enhancing their capacities as a positive global changemaker. [For those who are seeking a more scientific understanding of The Akashic Field, Dr Ervin Laszlo's *The Immutable Laws of The Akashic Field* is a recommended text, and readers may also find many useful resources on The Laszlo Institute website (https://thelaszloinstitute.com).]

Becoming Open to Guidance From The Akashic Records

In *The Akashic Records*, Sandra Anne Taylor identifies a number of actions that individuals can take in order to become more open to receiving guidance, useful information, or specific insights and assistance. Some key steps are as follows:

1. Open the mind to infinite possibilities.
2. Develop an attitude of being worthy and deserving of insights and assistance.
3. Meditate frequently in order to reach a level of consciousness that is willing to receive help (in whatever form it may manifest).
4. Use deep breathing techniques to physically relax, clear the mind, and completely let go (emotionally and mentally). Breath work can be further used to balance and centre energy, and to promote a sense of peace, calm, and tranquillity whilst setting intentions.
5. Focus on being heart-centred. Let go of negative mental activity (including judgement, worry, and anxiety) in order to become more connected to the heart. Visualise troubling thoughts drifting away like a cloud to enhance heart consciousness.
6. Let go of all fear and become comfortable with the power held in the etheric realm.
7. Be in the moment and trust in the process of connecting with a higher energy to receive inspiration and guidance at any time.
8. Make practical preparations for key life / world changes being sought (be they minor or major in scale).
9. Develop a sense of the eternal love that is vibrating deep within. Embrace all feelings of love and follow the light.
10. Be deeply connected to a higher energy source.

Forms of Awakening

Another way to start accessing greater insights whilst working to create a better world, is to understand that there are much larger cosmic forces that guide human lives. In *The Spiritual Awakening Guide,* Mary Mueller Shutan says that when an individual begins to awaken, they start to come into the service of a higher energy. The process of awakening (whether deliberate or unintentional) can also lead to peak experiences, such as a person perceiving how small they are in a truly vast universe whilst time becomes non-linear. These kinds of revelatory phenomena can result in a greater comprehension of how *every* time and place (realm or dimension) is actually existing in the present. Mueller Shutan claims that by accessing 'the void', an individual can actively work with time and space as if they are merely constructs, thereby deepening their understanding that all humans are always part of the whole. Many mystics subsequently describe coming to know of a greater collective intelligence as a state of 'bliss', which is often characterised by feeling more in sync with the flow of the universe.

There are several stages that people often go through in the course of awakening. For instance, at the outset, a large number of emotions may emerge as past traumas are processed. This releasing of energies out of the physical body is an important step for an individual to become a clear 'channel' (for instance, in the important task of working to create a better world). In complex or sudden awakenings, many blockages may surface simultaneously, and a transition can come in the form of a crisis and be extremely dramatic. Mueller Shutan explains that while this can be a confusing and overwhelming experience, it is essential that individuals not escape by using numbing substances. Instead, large amounts of time should be dedicated to crying and actively healing any difficult psychological and emotional issues that arise. She also says that gradual awakenings are somewhat easier in that they allow uncomfortable material to be progressively released in a calm and consciously consensual way. Regardless of what kind of awakening is experienced, an individual must work through layers to uncover their true selves, which then enables them to dissolve the confining and separating illusions of the world.

Through such techniques as meditation, stillness, and self-inquiry, it is possible to let go of stored wounds, destructive patterns, and negative thinking, as well as transcend conditioned reality. Engaging in this kind of inner work can lead to increased awareness and a greater focus on love, compassion, and oneness - which, in turn, results in the experience of a larger number of synchronicities and the reception of more guidance and insights on how to improve the world. Meanwhile, lesson loops occur when an individual is repeatedly confronted with the same kind of challenging people or traumatic situations. Effective paths to self-discovery can include a conscious clearing of blockages, or breaking free of repetitive loops by acting, thinking, and behaving differently. In this way, individuals can successfully learn key life lessons and move on to the next level of insight.

In the course of moving beyond social conditioning, many people may experience what is known as a 'dark night of the soul', in which they feel an intense sense of despair and depression because they are looking internally, coming out of denial, and actively taking responsibility for their part in what is happening at the collective level on planet Earth. At this stage, ego-based suicidal thoughts can emerge, so it is crucial to engage in extensive healing work in order to consciously establish one's ultimate life purpose. By making such a link, significant people and events will be magnetised to the individual in order to accelerate the unfolding of a greater plan to improve the world. After deconstructing the self / ego, it is possible to completely drop all illusions: to properly comprehend collective patterns and grasp the reality that it is the human mind that actively constructs the world and its conditions.

The Universal Laws

In her comprehensive and highly revelatory book *A Little Light on the Spiritual Laws*, Diana Cooper groups a large number of widely recognised universal laws into four different categories. Developing a deep understanding of these laws is a fundamentally empowering way that individuals can access important insights that will help them generate positive change in the world.

In the first section, concerning 'The Basic Laws of Life', Cooper states that the first law of the universe is 'As Above, So Below'. This law can be understood as pertaining to the way in which the higher realm and the metaphysical state are reflected on the physical plane, as well as the fact that greater forms of wisdom and love can always be accessed by souls on Earth in order to shape a positive reality. As such, to secure help from the higher energy at any time, an individual can enter into a state of love and ask for assistance in a clear and calm way (Request), then they must be open to the guidance arriving in any shape or form. Cooper also points out that it is most productive to focus on inviting the energy of what is really desired (because what people resist actually persists), and to be highly aware of the Law of Attraction in any act of creation. Essentially, humans magnetise situations and other people who have similar energy vibrations, so whenever life difficulties do emerge, they can be transformed by altering one's underlying (subconscious or unconscious) beliefs and processes. An extremely large number of books have been published about the Law of Attraction (Rhonda Byrne's *The Secret* probably being the most famous), and they often cover such topics as the power of the mind, positive affirmations, instant manifestation, and how to create vision boards to generate desired life changes. Some of these texts detail how to engage in the shallow attraction of material items for superficial reasons, but an increasingly dominant idea being presented in New Age circles is that the more globally beneficial an individual's intentions, the more assistance they will receive in actualising exactly what is being sought for the greater good. Indeed, Cooper argues that in order to experience personal growth, it is important to learn detachment (from physical objects, expectations of other people, limiting emotions and beliefs), and to instead embrace unconditional love.

The first part of *A Little Light on the Spiritual Laws* also explores some interconnected concepts related to the notion of 'As Within, So Without'. Cooper explains that everybody and everything is a mirror for what an individual likes and dislikes about themselves (Reflection), and, even more than this, what an individual sees in others (positive or negative) is actually a projection of an aspect of themselves. As such, an individual's external reality reflects their inner state, because the world brings them whatever they believe to be true. For major global change, then, there must be a fundamental alteration in how people think and act, and awareness and forward movement can be achieved by individuals coming out of a state of denial.

The second section of Cooper's text is devoted to 'The Laws of Creation' and features some extremely useful practical advice which can be effectively implemented when working to bring positive change to the world. For instance, she argues that an individual can always create their own reality by clearly focusing their thoughts, words, and actions / energy (that is, their attention) on what they wish to manifest. When a person commits to a higher purpose intention; raises their vibration; has total faith; and does whatever is required to make something happen, then a higher energy will align with them to actively help them realise their vision. Cooper also points out that, due to the Law of Flow, the universe is constantly shifting and expanding, so a person can consciously and deliberately release old and limiting behaviours, emotions, and thoughts in order to generate a preferred life. Cooper brings a very ethical dimension to the creation of qualities like abundance, prosperity, and success. She advocates that all forms of money, resources, and personal skills must be utilised in responsible ways; that the individual should open up to receiving higher qualities like love and happiness, as well as actively bring them into the lives of others; and that success is actually about having the integrity to work without ego on achieving the highest good for all.

'The Laws of Higher Awareness' are detailed in the third part of the book, and many of the concepts are common to a range of spiritual practices and faiths. For instance, Cooper discusses the purpose of reincarnation, whereby recurring issues can be resolved by seeking the light (love), engaging in healing, and learning key life lessons. Spiritually noble and virtuous actions can also help to generate good karma or eliminate bad karma. Favoured pursuits like meditation, prayer, and affirmation are further outlined by Cooper. Being still, quietening the mind, and having positive intentions are paramount to receiving useful ideas, insightful feedback, and quality guidance during any act of internal or external creation (especially whilst generating positive change in the world). In order to come to a state of higher awareness, Cooper identifies several concepts that individuals must master on the Earth plane. For example, a person will be regarded as being ready for greater things when they are able to view challenges and responsibilities as an honour rather than a negative inconvenience. Humans also need to learn how to listen to, and be guided by, their own intuitive voice so that they can practise discernment and gain greater forms of wisdom. Ultimately, each person should be aiming to achieve balance by using centring to bring their opposing aspects into equilibrium.

Finally, the fourth part of Diana Cooper's publication documents 'The Laws of Higher Frequency'. In this section, Cooper explains that energy is vibrating at different frequencies, and negative energies (like jealousy and guilt) are 'heavy' vibrations and 'low' in frequency, while positive energies (like love and joy) are 'light' and 'high'. She says that all individuals can raise their energy vibrations by being honest and optimistic; frequently expressing gratitude (especially for significant challenges); and living a healthy life. In this way, people can physically heal; resolve difficult emotional issues; and actively work to create a better world for themselves and others. In line with the notion of energetic interconnectedness is the idea of 'oneness', in which everything and everyone is part of the same source. Since duality, separation, and differentiation are mere illusions, all people and situations should thus be viewed without judgement. An individual's level of consciousness further allows things to be seen from multiple perspectives and, hence, in a non-judgemental way. Meanwhile, practising compassion, unconditional love, and forgiveness (instruments of grace) can be an effective path to personal healing and freedom from karma. In terms of assisting the planet, Cooper explains how certain 'Higher Frequency Laws' can be activated to ensure success. For example, blessings and miracles can be dispensed when an individual makes a decree and a commitment to co-create something socially important from a place of integrity; when genuine requests are humbly made; when they are on their true path; and when they replace fear and doubt with complete faith (connecting to inner guidance and trusting synchronicities).

Soul Lessons and Life Purpose

In a similar fashion, Sonia Choquette channels information about twenty-two 'soul lessons' that humans come to the Earth plane to learn. Striving to master these lessons are, then, a way for people to connect to higher energy insights and guidance whilst working to create a better world. In her book *Soul Lessons and Soul Purpose*, Choquette divides the lessons into two categories: 'Learning to Use Your Creative Power' and 'Working With Divine Law'.

In the section concerning how humans can effectively acquire the required knowledge to utilise their innate creativity for the greater good, Choquette explains that an individual must first recognise their immortality and true power. Fundamental to this power is the ability of all individuals to work in combination with a higher energy to generate everything that is happening in the world. This means, then, that every person is co-creating the circumstances of their own lives and that of the planet as a whole. People must also fully comprehend that the process of manifestation originates in the mind and is intentional. In other words, creation begins with thought and imagination equals energy. After any original conception needs to come desire, which is an emotion that has to arise in order for ideas to become fully realised. Another major claim from Choquette's channelled sources is that humans best create by utilising pictures (rather than words), as providing the subconscious mind with clear images empowers it to bring all visions into reality. Also key to successful creation is actively choosing to live in the present, since the ability to manifest things exists only in the now (this is because the past cannot be altered, and the future can only be shaped by current actions). A particularly important concept that all people on Earth must come to proper terms with is that the act of creating requires no contribution whatsoever from the personal ego. According to the insights documented by Choquette, creation is simply a process of channelling from the higher self, and creativity flows more freely when individuals are able to transcend their egos. Ultimately, by being receptive; living with an open heart; following inner wisdom (rather than superficial ego demands); and utilising deeper awareness derived from logic (reason) and objective thinking, an individual can become filled with positive energy and work at achieving the greatest good for all. Choquette ends this section with a lesson about detachment, which concerns the fact that happiness should be dependent on the quality of one's greater life purpose rather than attachment to the physical world or material things.

In the second section, Choquette provides detailed information about the concept of 'divine order'. The argument is that, before incarnating on Earth, souls choose the order of their life experiences so that they are provided with progressive opportunities for psychological, emotional, and spiritual growth. For instance, sometimes people are required to reverse their perceptions or shift their awareness in order to evolve, and they can do this by drawing on higher energy support in order to transform any situation (including turning negative world realities into positive ones). Another lesson concerns the importance of surrendering all forms of self-importance and narcissism (ego) in order to serve the greater good of creating a better world. Essentially, the soul advances towards mastery by facing, and overcoming, a wide range of challenges (trials, tribulations, or tests), and life obstacles can be more easily and rapidly surmounted when fully embraced and dealt with in a willing, humble, and joyful manner. As part of this, individuals can become more fully empowered by taking personal responsibility for their faults, flaws, errors, and wrongdoings. An effective way to do this is by consistently engaging in admissions and corrections. Meanwhile, repeated issues (problematic patterns) are a result of negative thinking and behaviours, and can be actively replaced with positive thoughts and actions by retraining the mind and breaking unproductive habits. Choquette's channelled material also indicates that while 'time' is really only an Earthly concept, an individual can experience greater forms of evolution if it spends its days engaging in acts of integrity and helping the world to become a fairer and most just place. In addition, the latter part of *Soul Lessons and Soul Purpose* features some highly practical suggestions, including to actively meditate, because people manifest what they focus on, so conscious meditation can be a path to the creation of a preferred life and world.

Astrological Insights

Many people understand the importance of knowing their Western astrological chart and the dominance of Earth, Fire, Water, or Air in their Zodiac Signs (Sun, Moon, Venus, and Mars) in terms of what life interests, paths, and roles they pursue. The Chinese horoscope and Indian astrological systems can also provide invaluable guidance for individuals in the course of making key choices and decisions regarding who they are and what they are doing on planet Earth. For instance, by using Vedic Astrology, a person can determine both their South Node (relating to past life and its influence on present life circumstances) and their North Node (relating to destiny). According to *Astrostyle*, the South Node provides insight into the challenges and talents that a soul has carried with them from previous lifetimes. The North Node, meanwhile, is relevant to karmic paths; the lessons that a person came to Earth to learn; the particular body (or bodies) of knowledge that an individual is acquiring in a given lifetime; and each soul's ultimate planetary purpose (including the creation of a better world for all of humanity).

*Diana Cooper's *A Little Light on the Spiritual Laws* and Sonia Choquette's *Soul Lessons and Soul Purpose* are both extremely detailed yet highly accessible books, full of illuminating metaphors, insightful examples, and relatable anecdotes. This chapter's brief summary of their key ideas does neither of the works proper justice, so readers are encouraged to access and read these texts in full so as to gain a deeper understanding of the identified concepts.

---

*As previously noted, Part 2 features information from a wide range of theoretical perspectives (including language and concepts from New Age, Mystical, Esoteric, and Metaphysical texts that many people wary of spiritual beliefs may find problematic). Since this section is about 'cutting-edge ideas' and personal empowerment, it is important to again emphasise that maintaining an open mind and finding commonalities and unity in diverse beliefs may, in itself, be a path to creating a better world. [Additional research is encouraged - please refer to Appendix B and the Bibliography.]

PART 3:

EMPOWERING AGENTS OF POSITIVE WORLD CHANGE THROUGH PERSONAL WELL-BEING ACTIVITIES

Chapter 9: Physical Well-Being Activities
- Adopt a Healthy Diet
- Have Adequate Amounts of Quality Sleep
- Engage in Breath Work and Regular Exercise
- Pursue Non-Materialism and Decluttering
- Disconnect From Technology
- Clean Personal and Public Spaces
- Clear Energetic Fields
- Favour Natural Healing Methods
- Utilise Earth's Healing Energies
- Create Positive Physical Environments

Chapter 10: Mental Well-Being Activities
- Be Honest
- Bring Unconscious Material Into the Conscious Mind
- Use Meditation and Words of Great Resonance to Break Unproductive Mental Patterns
- Laugh Regularly
- Alter the Mindset to Clear Negative Energies: Use Mental Discipline to Engage in Positive Thinking
- Transcend the Ego State
- Engage in Deep Reflection Then Focus on the Present
- Make Moving Forward the End Goal
- Be Open-Minded and Non-Judgemental

Chapter 11: Emotional Well-Being Activities
- Learn Relevant Lessons From Disrespectful People and Harmful Situations Then Evolve Beyond Them
- Heal Emotionally by Holding Self and Others to Account
- Clear Deep Trauma, Multiple Levels of Emotional Pain, and Problematic Patterns
- Objectively Respond to Life Challenges
- Appreciate Nature's Cycles as a Path to Emotional Healing
- Engage in Random Acts of Kindness or Become a Volunteer
- Give Up Toxic Aspects of Western Society
- Develop an Attitude of Gratitude

CHAPTER 9
PHYSICAL WELL-BEING ACTIVITIES

When embarking on any personal empowerment path in order to be an agent of positive world change, there are a number of steps that can be taken on a practical level. Such activities aim to reduce physiological, psychological, and emotional stress, thereby making it easier for the individual to maintain a maximum level of health, well-being, and energy. The following information details physical choices that individuals can make in order to enhance their ability to enact beneficial change in the world.

Adopt a Healthy Diet

The human body functions in the healthiest and most efficient way when it is provided with a nutritious diet. Processing toxins puts the body under a great deal of stress and depletes people of life-giving energy. Increasing intake of a wide variety of fresh fruit and vegetables, and decreasing consumption of salt and highly processed and refined foods like sugar is universally recommended. Raw nuts, seeds, legumes, and wholegrains are frequently cited as being valuable components of a healthy diet. Adequate intake of calcium and iron (either through dairy and lean red meat, or other plant-based and protein sources) is also essential. Eating to suit one's individual body and only engaging in moderate consumption is common sense advice for maintaining appropriate weight and good overall health. Consuming suitable portion sizes and nutritious foods are, then, key to a diet that assists with optimal physical functioning. [*See Appendix C for more detailed dietary guidelines and healthy eating recommendations.]

Stimulants like caffeine, and toxins and poisons like alcohol, cigarettes, and drugs put the body under enormous duress (due to the additional processing functions that have to be activated), and they create artificial cravings that detract from overall energy. [*See Appendix D for additional information regarding the harmful physical and psychological effects of drugs and alcohol.] A poor diet that is high in 'junk' food and low in essential vitamins and minerals further impedes mental functioning and learning ability. When individuals are physically unwell and operating at reduced mental capacity, they are also prone to becoming emotionally strained and unbalanced. As such, it is essential to eliminate all artificial and addictive substances from one's diet (daily intake) and life in general. A regular physical cleanse (or detox) can be a useful strategy for re-establishing good habits. Ultimately, a consistently healthy body is always desirable because it can maximise personal energy and assist an individual to be a more effective agent of social change.

Have Adequate Amounts of Quality Sleep

Essential to any kind of sustained physical well-being is regular and adequate amounts of sleep. Both the body and mind must have frequent access to quality deep sleep in order to ensure peak functioning. There are a wide range of strategies that individuals can employ to ensure they are getting the right amount of sleep to meet their personal operational needs. Eric Suni (*OneCare Media*) suggests:

- going to bed at the same time every night (or only when truly tired) and waking up at the same time every morning;
- making the bedroom (and house) quiet and peaceful (minimising external forms of noise wherever possible);
- establishing clear routines before going to bed (such as having a warm bath or brushing one's teeth);
- setting up a physical environment that is conducive to sleep (a comfortable mattress and pillow, and bedding that does not cause over-heating or coldness);
- engaging in deep breathing and meditation in order to physically relax and clear the mind of anxious thoughts;
- exercising early in the day;
- consistently balancing work, play, and sleep hours each day (this may involve avoiding jobs that require double shifts, night shifts, or over-time);
- regularly masturbating or having mutually satisfying sex with a loyal and caring partner;
- ensuring that no stimulants (like sugar, caffeine, nicotine, alcohol, and drugs), heavy meals, or diuretics are consumed close to bed time (digestive issues, dehydration, or the need to frequently urinate can significantly interfere with sustained sleep);
- avoiding irregular forms of extended napping (especially late in the day);

- winding down by disconnecting from visual and intellectual sources for half an hour prior to sleep (including not reading, talking on the phone, watching television, or using technological devices);
- increasing fruit and vegetable consumption whilst decreasing excess meat intake;
- exposing oneself to sunlight during the day and no forms of artificial light when in bed at night; and
- balancing fluid intake prior to sleep (enough to prevent waking up to drink water during the night, but not so much as to result in excessive urination).

Quality sleep is essential for maximising personal health, well-being, and the energy levels needed to be a committed agent of positive world change.

Engage in Breath Work and Regular Exercise

One of the quickest and most effective ways to deal with feelings of anxiety or stress is to engage in conscious breathing. In the course of focusing intently on body and breath, an individual can more easily let go of upsetting thoughts and physical discomfort. By using a wide variety of breathing exercises, it is possible to generate different outcomes. For instance, deep intakes of fresh air and slow exhales through the mouth allow lungs to be cleared of all staleness. This in turn assists with oxygenation of the brain and the ability to think more clearly and positively. Most meditative practices also incorporate controlled breathing as part of the path to physical and mental relaxation, followed by more advanced soul work.

Another important component of good health and optimal physical functioning (including strength and flexibility) is regular exercise that does not put the body at risk of injury, or the mind exposed to inherently negative qualities like competitiveness. Non-competitive or spiritually-oriented exercise practices include Tai Chi; Feldenkrais / Integrated Awareness; Yoga; Qigong (for breath work); dancing for fun; and nature-based forms of walking / hiking, swimming, and surfing. Spiritually-connected forms of sex (inspired by genuine love and care) can also be important for optimal physical and psychological well-being. When the body is fit and strong, it is better able to support a healthy mental and emotional state, and this frees the individual energetically so that it can focus on generating desirable global change in a more efficient way.

Pursue Non-Materialism and Decluttering

All material items carry physical energy. This can take the form of personal memories; environmental implications (pollution, resource depletion, and threats to animal welfare being just some of the energetic consequences of the widescale manufacture of material goods); and the emotional and psychological imprints of those who have created the products while working in inhumane or hostile conditions. One theory of Feng Shui is that material possessions are always communicating or interacting with their owners on an energetic level. Excessive amounts of physical energy in personal environments can therefore work to clutter thoughts and distract individuals from any important tasks which aim to create a better world. Obviously, the more possessions a person has, the more exhausted they can become in having to deal with all the energies circulating their home (not to mention the copious amount of time that has to be dedicated to cleaning, organising, and storing such material items). Many experts also regard acts of hoarding (including keeping any object that has not been utilised in the past twelve months) as akin to obesity. In other words, both hoarders and over-eaters are attempting to fill some kind of 'hole' – be it because of a significant loss experienced in life, or because of an emotional gap one is trying to 'plug up'.

A large number of mystics, spiritual seekers, and leaders have taken vows of poverty, dedicating their lives and souls to explorations of the divine rather than the acquisition of money and material items. Given that climate change is primarily being attributed to the greenhouse gas emissions resulting from post-World War II consumption in Western countries, humanity now has both a moral and spiritual duty to massively reduce purchase of material goods. Where home, work, social, and even natural environments are increasingly full of manufactured products, people should seek to engage in decluttering exercises. This can include donating all objects that carry old energies to charity; removing plastics from oceans and beaches; using up food in kitchen pantries that may go to waste through expiry; and repurposing, regifting, or recycling everything that is no longer used or required for survival. By not engaging in the acquisition or hoarding of money and goods, and by removing all unnecessary material items from daily living, it is possible to eliminate unproductively distracting forms of energy, thereby allowing a greater focus on issues of environmentalism, equity, peace, and justice.

Disconnect From Technology

An increasing number of studies are showing that the dominance of technology in the lives of many contemporary peoples is partially responsible for alarming growths in obesity, as well as massive spikes in feelings of anxiety and a range of more serious health issues (including clinical depression and a variety of eating disorders). The addictive nature of gaming and social media use - or simply being constantly online / digitally connected via mobile phones - is raising multiple concerns about the well-being of greater humanity. While short-term 'digital detoxes' are becoming increasingly popular, individuals would also be well served by massively reducing the amount of time spent on digital devices every single day. According to Kendra Cherry (*Very Well Mind*), the benefits of disconnecting from technology include:
- reduced stress and anxiety levels;
- improved sleep quantity and quality;
- enhanced intuitive and creative abilities;
- deepened connections with other humans (via real-life social interactions and conversations);
- increased opportunities for exercise (and the positive health, fitness, and weight effects resulting from additional physical movement);
- more time to spend with animals and exploring natural environments; and
- the ability to focus on being fully present and happy in each moment (rather than feeling dissatisfied, jealous, or obsessed with past relationships whilst using social media).

Whenever possible, then, people should completely turn off all technological devices. The physical health benefits and positive energy generated from doing so can significantly increase an individual's personal happiness, as well as their ability to create beneficial change in the world. Reducing the distracting chimes of constant (and often very shallow) social media notifications can also allow extra time to pursue more environmentally friendly forms of societal change.

Clean Personal and Public Spaces

Thoroughly cleaning all personal environments can significantly raise energy levels, because most humans positively respond to open, light, airy, and fully cleansed spaces. In the process of washing or dusting it is possible to quite literally remove all the 'gunk' and dirt from personal physical realms – a symbolic act that has great psychological resonance as the mind comes to feel cleaner, clearer, and as having enough space to accommodate the new. Most people know how much lighter and better they feel after a haircut, shower, or shave, as well as the positive feelings that flood the body following a big Spring Clean. Just as Spring signifies the end of a cold and bleak time (Winter), so too can cleaning the home, living environment, work station, storage unit, car, or garden mark the completion of dark periods, and a greater movement into bringing beneficial change.

Voluntarily engaging in the cleaning of public environments is also important, as it promotes calm and positive human interactions (indeed, there seems to be a high correlation between the prevalence of social angst / violence and dirty or neglected urban environments). Programmes like Tidy Towns and annual nationwide Clean Up events that focus on removing rubbish and reducing pollution are thus of enormous benefit to both nature and wider humanity. Ultimately, physical cleaning can be associated with deeper forms of psychological, emotional, and spiritual cleansing (for the individual, as well as whole communities and societies), and can subsequently create preferred global realities.

Clear Energetic Fields

In her highly practical book *Black is the New Light,* Rebecca Campbell identifies a number of strategies that individuals can employ to protect, replenish, and clear their energetic field, and thereby raise their vibrations to better generate positivity in the world. Through visualisation activities, it is also possible to clear the energy fields of others who may be seeking healing.

1. Bathe in Salts

Many salts are suitable for cleansing the energetic field through a process of physical detoxification and balancing.

2. Transmute Bad Energy Via Nature (for example, Earthing)

Various parts of nature (the ground, the trunk of a tree) can be physically connected with to dissolve or release negativity, and for a person to be subsequently recharged with positive healing energy from the Earth frequency.

3. Protect Personal Energy Fields

Since life on this planet is frequently characterised by the need to deal with challenging people and surmount diverse obstacles, it is common for individuals to feel drained. Campbell suggests that personal energy can be protected by visualising a large bubble of bright white light surrounding the physical body, or by imagining an energetic space of one to two metres between the self and others.

4. Take a Chakra Shower

Various forms of Hinduism and Buddhism regard the human body as having 'wheels of energy' known as chakras which are located as follows: crown of the head (violet); between the eyebrows (indigo); throat (blue); heart (green); navel (yellow); root of the sexual organs (orange); and base of the spine (red). In the course of living life on the energy-dense Earth plane, the chakras (which are associated with different emotions) can become blocked or stagnant. This often occurs when an individual is required to process particularly difficult emotions like grief, rage, or intense loneliness. A daily 'chakra shower' is therefore suggested, as an individual can imagine all stuck energy being washed away while water runs over separate parts of the body. After cleansing, each chakra can then be visualised as being filled with luminous white light (Source energy), or a shaft of light in the symbolically relevant colour (for instance, green light for a heart which has been broken by a deceitful or unfaithful partner).

5. Cut Problematic Cords

Invisible energetic cords provide a connection between people, and while many of these may be gentle or flexible, and hence positive, in nature (taking the form of a ribbon or piece of elastic, for example), others can be extremely problematic and draw excessive amounts of energy from an individual. Negative cord connections may operate more like hooks, ropes, or steel cables (due to the acts of blackmail, jealousy, manipulation, or guilt being invoked by the relationship), and can work to seriously deplete the energy levels of both parties. Campbell suggests that individuals tune in to their bodies at the end of each day, then take note of where each cord is attached (the chakra) and what each is made of. After this, she recommends visualising the cutting of these cords with whatever instrument or tool is required to complete the task - be it scissors, wire cutters, a knife, or a big sword.

Actively removing blocked or difficult energies from one's life can subsequently create more space, time, and motivation to work on important tasks associated with creating a better world.

Favour Natural Healing Methods

Western medications are often addictive and have a wide variety of negative side-effects, so use of natural healing methods should always be considered whenever possible. Where practices like reiki; massage; acupuncture; crystal healing; emotional clearing; positive thinking / affirmations; or herbal, mineral, vitamin, and food remedies prove effective, they should be favoured for their gentler impact on the physical body. An increasing number of studies into the far-reaching health benefits of individual and collective meditation (often referred to as Group Consciousness), and the scientifically accepted placebo effect provide extensive evidence that the mind is able to exercise power over the body and promote less invasive forms of healing.

The Dutch author Wim Hof (*The Wim Hof Method*) advocates a three-pillared approach to increasing personal energy; decreasing stress; strengthening the immune system (thereby eliminating many forms of pain and illness); ensuring better quality sleep; improving cognitive ability and physical performance; enhancing mood; losing weight; alleviating anxiety; and maximising the ability to survive in challenging and extreme environments. Hof claims that contemporary humans need to reawaken physiological processes that were dominant in ancestral times (that is, when people spent more time in external, natural environments). He argues that through cold exposure (such as by taking regular cold showers); conscious breathing (via repeated deep breathing cycles); and consistent development of the power of the mind, anybody can engage in complete forms of physical control and self-healing. Ultimately, optimal health and reduced physical stress helps to empower individuals to become more effective and energetic agents of positive world change.

Utilise Earth's Healing Energies

In *Runes*, Andy Baggott has written extensively about the notion that various places on Earth have a strong and vibrant energy which is powerful enough to alter human consciousness and provide profound forms of physical healing. Ley lines are paths along which the energy system of the Earth flows. Some of their points are close to the surface and can be prime places for the occurrence of synchronicities, revelations, miracles (like instant healing), and effective spiritual work (such as balancing energies). Many ancient peoples believed that forming circles in these spots helped to harness energy, hence the presence of stone circles all around the world (the most famous example being Stone Henge). Also, since rocks take millions of years to form, it is believed that they hold ancient bodies of Earth wisdom and knowledge, as well as great levels of energetic power and strength. Sacred stone / rock sites (like Uluru in Australia's Northern Territory) are therefore protected as the keepers of great and old wisdom, and regarded as spiritually powerful places where difficult thoughts and emotions can be cleared through open and honest soul work.

Similarly, crystals can be used by humans to generate specific forms of clearing and physical healing, or to attract certain kinds of energies and life experiences (including taking consistent action to create a better world). In *The Practical Guide to Crystal Healing*, Marc James and Dhyan Klein claim that clear crystals can be utilised to manifest dynamic energy, while milky crystals work to promote nurturing energy. They regard quartz crystals as particularly powerful in terms of being able to store vibrations; stimulate personal energies; assist with goal completion; and bring visions, awareness, and clarity. James and Klein also identify a number of qualities associated with specific crystals that agents of positive world change might like to draw on. These include:

- Rose Quartz – attracts love, compassion, emotional connection, and wisdom;
- Apophyllite – facilitates connection to the higher self and universal intelligence;
- Chrysoprase – awakens psychic abilities;
- Garnet – regenerates the physical body;
- Lapis Lazuli – activates intuition and dissolves unconscious mental blocks;
- Malachite – releases suppressed emotions;
- Obsidian – breaks down old forms of psychological conditioning and restrictive patterns;

- Turquoise – amplifies healing energy and promotes good physical health; and
- Tourmaline – cleanses and transmutes blockages into positive energy.

More detailed and complete lists of crystals and their associated qualities are widely available from a range of New Age sources (stores, books, and online articles), but it is also worth investigating contemporary scientific understandings of the energetic power held within crystal structures. [NB Individuals purchasing crystals should ensure that they have been sourced in highly ethical ways.]

Create Positive Physical Environments

There are a range of other physical level choices that individuals can make in order to generate positive personal environments and thereby enhance their ability to change the world in beneficial ways. Some strategies include:
- regularly nurturing self with love and care (this can involve engaging in self-forgiveness when big life mistakes are made, or ensuring that personal protection and safety are always paramount);
- spending time in locations with positive associations (as well as actively avoiding places that have negative energies or cause problematic memories to repeatedly emerge); and
- choosing healthy and joyous social interactions (including ending contact with people who generate unpleasant dramas and demeaning situations).

Ultimately, maximising physical health and clearing negative energies are highly effective ways that individuals can become more empowered, and thus better able to work at improving the world.

CHAPTER 10
MENTAL WELL-BEING ACTIVITIES

For optimal mental health and functioning (and therefore an increased ability to be an agent of positive world change), it is important to reduce constant forms of stress that are negative in nature, and to instead seek out situations and human interactions that provide positive intellectual stimulation. There are multiple strategies for clearing stress and negativity that individuals can adopt.

Be Honest
Every time an individual tells a lie they generate high levels of psychological stress. Feelings of personal discord; shame; and fear of being found out are frequently experienced, as well as a great sense of pressure due to a perceived need to weave an elaborate web of associated lies just to maintain the original deceit. There is also often an engagement in massive amounts of mental activity in an effort to provide a sense of self-justification as to why the lie has been told.

Sometimes wider society puts individuals in extremely difficult situations where they feel forced to lie - as was the case for people hiding Jews in Nazi Germany, or for homosexuals who live in countries where they face the death penalty for their natural sexual practices. Also, on occasions it is actually 'polite' to lie rather than create a stressful drama. For instance, a person's father-in-law may have a mental illness that causes him to explode with anger when honestly told how rude he is, so simply smiling and being tolerant of his obnoxious behaviours in order to keep the peace can be regarded as a way of expressing love and support for one's partner. In spite of certain exceptions, there are, however, many strong arguments for being bluntly honest and holding difficult people to account for their offensive comments and actions, as this may be the only way to confront and transform discriminatory and harmful attitudes in wider society.

Wherever possible, it is beneficial for the soul to express its ultimate truth, then leave those locations and situations where there is pressure to lie. Pursuing the path of complete honesty is best for ensuring maximum mental harmony and complete personal well-being. Thus, for those individuals who have engaged in consistent, protracted, or highly complicated forms of lying, a process of making amends may be the right path to follow for personal and public redemption, as well as release from any resultant forms of mental anguish. Ultimately, it is psychologically clear and healthy individuals who are best able to generate positive forms of change in a distraught world.

Bring Unconscious Material Into the Conscious Mind

Just as important as being honest with the outside world, is being totally honest with self. This can often be an incredibly difficult process, as the conscious mind routinely works to keep the individual in a state of denial in order to protect the ego. While this may reduce personal levels of stress in the short term, ultimately the unconscious mind will work to sabotage everything that the individual has worked to project at the ego level in order to force them to confront the truth. The processes of self-sabotage that most people experience (such as in the form of life crises) can result in extremely high levels of stress (and suicidal thoughts), however psychological wholeness and happiness (and thus a more lasting elimination of deep mental stress) can be achieved when the individual is able to consciously hold themselves to account and acknowledge everything in a brutally honest way.

For instance, a person may have become a teacher in order to educate Westerners about systemic forms of racism faced by Indigenous peoples, however in the course of working in government schools they are required to label many students as 'very low achievers' (in official reporting processes) as a result of the latter's struggles to write coherent essays in the invading language of English. As a consequence of receiving payment for grading and ranking First Nations pupils as 'failures', the teacher develops a deep-seated guilt complex that results in them developing a personal relationship with a young Indigenous man who dropped out of school (due to constantly feeling like he is academically worthless), and who is frequently engaging in heavy drug use. In the course of regularly cleaning up his drug-related legal messes, the teacher is forced to acknowledge that they are often acting as his enabler, whilst also playing out their own white guilt issues when trying to express love. By consciously acknowledging the unconscious motivations and machinations that have been driving the relationship, the teacher can free themselves of the extreme levels of negativity and stress characterising their personal and professional life, and then start to properly address systemic racism at the macrocosmic level. This in turn allows their life blueprint to unfold and, ultimately, a more positive and successful fulfilling of their greater life purpose to occur.

It is important to always see hardship as a spiritual gift (or a great blessing in disguise), and to not be afraid to embrace both the 'ups' and 'downs' of life's experience. Indeed, at key times it is crucial to learn how to survive extreme difficulty so that one can develop the essential skills of knowing how to transform the self from wounded victim to strong warrior in any trying situation. Developing a self-perception as a survivor can often be the first step in letting go of those repetitive thoughts and behavioural patterns that are commonly related to having a victim mentality. By seeing life as cyclical (rather than linear) in nature, it is possible to understand that individuals are required to face increasingly difficult challenges (often circling around similar themes or issues) as they mature. Each 'crisis' is an opportunity to demonstrate an increasing ability to deal with trying situations in a calm, psychologically aware, and gracious manner.

Even at those points when an individual's entire identity is being challenged, it is still possible to experience a sense of internal happiness as one's self-knowledge grows, and 'dark' times can actually be interpreted as a period of rest and renewal for better days ahead. The best path forward is to not fear or resist change and what the future holds – everything that happens is a crucial part of life's journey, and it is a mark of wisdom if an individual is able to acknowledge the spiritual advancement that lies in the experience of negative (as well as positive) life events. As with the Yin and Yang philosophy, in every seemingly 'bad' situation there is some good (and vice versa). Ultimately, people are always sowing the seeds of their own crises and healings (the two processes are deeply interconnected), and these psychological journeys are fundamentally linked to realisation of one's life purpose and coming to a greater conception of how they can create a better world.

Use Meditation and Words of Great Resonance to Break Unproductive Mental Patterns

An increasing number of academic studies have provided scientific support for the centuries-old practice of using meditation to reduce physical stress and train the mind (or actually 'rewire'

the brain) to have more positive thoughts and spiritually-connected insights. In *Breaking the Habit of Being Yourself*, Joe Dispenza argues that by relaxing the body and calming the mind (or altering the brain's wave state), humans are able to achieve a wide range of highly beneficial life modifications, including:
- seeing difficult situations from a fresh perspective (subsequently allowing an individual to find effective new solutions for old dramas);
- signalling a desire that the higher self find efficient ways to resolve bad habits and unproductive patterns of mind (such as a self-pitying victim mentality); and
- realising ways to shift stagnant and damaging energies (which can involve changing negative life scenarios and consequently engaging in deeper forms of psychological healing).

Meditation is often described as a process of letting go of an attachment to the repetitive (or obsessive) thoughts that fill the mind. Proponents of mindfulness claim that by simply observing thoughts as they pass by, they lose their emotional power and it is possible to find more objective ways to solve problematic life issues.

Being language-based creatures, humans also frequently find words of great comfort in times of grief, pain, or difficulty. These can be:
- wise words in the form of advice from family, friends, and mentors;
- quotes from the famous and insightful;
- affirmations / brief statements used to stay positive and focused on new goals; or
- mantras or single words / phrases used in the course of meditation in order to focus the mind and allow release of persistent and troubling thoughts.

'Om' is probably the most utilised word for mantras (or at least the most famous one favoured for its sound of 'the universe' or 'divinity'), while affirmations often take the form of 'gratitude' and 'attraction' statements. Affirmations are meant to be short so that they can be regularly repeated throughout the course of a day and before sleep at night. In this way, positive goals can seep into the subconscious, and the unconscious mind can subsequently be activated to find ways to manifest them in the real world. Example affirmations could be structured using key phrases like, 'I give thanks for…' and 'I ask for guidance in attracting (or manifesting) love / abundance / contentment / health / happiness / intellectual stimulation / wisdom / freedom [or whatever is most desired]'. Both meditation and positive words can be used, then, to free the mind of negative preoccupations and stresses, and to generate a greater sense of peace, calm, and spiritual awareness to allow more effective engagement in social change processes.

Laugh Regularly

Laughter is a key way to bring increased amounts of positive energy into everyday life. The act of laughing can also provide an important balance during times of difficulty or grief (that is, when a person may be experiencing an intense shedding of tears). Daily laughter is an excellent way to release pent-up tension and suppressed emotions, and it works as a reminder that feelings of pure joy are always possible. Even during one's bleakest times, simply forcing laughter can create a physiological change and the happiness chemicals released into the brain (that is, dopamine, serotonin, endorphins, and oxytocin) greatly enhance psychological well-being. Many relaxation centres run workshops dedicated to groups of people gathering to laugh. Alternatively, individuals can sit quietly and replay hilarious memories and conversations in their minds until they are smiling broadly or laughing out loud. If there are no past interactions or experiences that give rise to mirth, it is possible to imagine funny scenarios, or make up amusing dialogue to generate laughter. Lying down and forcibly doing belly laughs can work as an amazing mood enhancer as well.

Regularly reading humorous books, listening to witty song lyrics, or watching film and television comedies can be a further way to stimulate laughter and promote happy thoughts. Indeed, one theory is that an individual's state of mind can be determined by a survey of the last five cultural forms they have engaged with. Entertainment selections not only reflect how someone is seeing the world, but they overtly influence or actively shape personal levels of contentment and well-being (negative social media commentaries should thus be avoided at all times). Playing with pets or caring friends can be another source of genuine, stress-relieving laughter. For anybody who is being plagued by negative thoughts - and is consequently having trouble connecting to feelings of love and higher level guidance - the answer may simply be to intentionally and repeatedly laugh until all the pain is gone and the channel to wisdom is clear. Agents of significant world change can then work more effectively and make a bigger impact when they are operating with a positive frame of mind.

Alter the Mindset to Clear Negative Energies: Use Mental Discipline to Engage in Positive Thinking

Since it is not always possible to enter into the meditative state in the course of daily life, another strategy for releasing stress and maintaining a high vibrational state is to train the mind to turn all negative thoughts into positive ones. There are many physical signs to indicate when an individual's energies are in a negative or blocked state: hunched shoulders; frown wrinkles; and cloudy eyes to name a few. According to Penney Peirce (*The Intuitive Way*), other signs that a person needs to engage in some serious energy clearing activities include that they are:

- regularly focusing on or thinking about the past;
- feeling stressed, anxious, or overwhelmed;
- lacking in clear direction;
- feeling lethargic, unmotivated, depressed, or confused;
- experiencing low confidence and self-esteem, or a sense of self-loathing;
- being constantly misunderstood, misinterpreted, or ignored; and
- believing that everything is 'falling apart' (as a result of losing several things, having consistent bad luck and frequent accidents, or attracting regular incidences of being exploited and defrauded).

In order to clear such blockages, it is essential that an individual alters their entire mindset: their beliefs, attitudes, and thinking habits. For instance, in *Stop the Excuses!*, Wayne Dyer claims that self-sabotaging thoughts like, 'I can't change because...it will be too difficult / I can't afford it / I can't do it on my own / I'm too old / I'm too busy / I'm too scared / I don't have the energy', will keep a person energetically blocked and deeply unhappy. If, instead, people reverse their habits of mind and develop a positive attitude and central belief that they can do or achieve anything, then their energies will quickly become unblocked, and they will move forward into a happier and healthier life.

Even when an individual is undoubtedly facing incredibly difficult and challenging life circumstances, it is still possible to 'find the cloud's silver lining', or, as another old cliché goes, 'take lemons and turn them into lemonade'. With hindsight, many people also say that the 'worst' thing that ever happened to them eventually turned out to be the best thing that ever happened to them. By disciplining the mind to stop automatically interpreting certain events in a negative way, one can instead see everything as an *opportunity* for a much better and more positive reality. By not expending excessive amounts of energy on obsessively revisiting negative thoughts, an individual can also free up a great deal of mental space for determining how to rapidly move out of undesirable situations and into more positive realities. As well, sometimes simply changing perspectives can alert an individual to the fact that they are not actually dissatisfied with their current circumstances at all – many very fortunate and privileged people frequently find the most trivial things to complain about and to subsequently put them in a completely unjustified bad mood. At such times it is worth remembering that there are no doubt millions (if not billions) of people in the world who are facing more trying life hardships. Focusing attention on how to genuinely help alleviate world hunger, the global refugee crisis, or the widescale destruction of many rainforests, can relieve much narcissistic pondering of microcosmic level issues that are quite unimportant in the overall scheme of things.

In the course of transforming one's thinking, it is also useful to consider some of the world's most inspiring individuals who have managed to turn the toughest forms of injustice into meaningful personal journeys that have had global resonance. Nelson Mandela spent a phenomenal twenty-seven years incarcerated in South Africa, yet came to embrace peace on both a personal level and in his subsequent presidential role that signified the official end of Apartheid in that country. Meanwhile, many survivors of sexual assault and violence (such as former slaves in North America) have become advocates for international legal reforms that provide fundamental protections for less empowered peoples around the globe. There are, as well, countless stories of individuals who have been diagnosed as having terminal illnesses and have gone on to use the power of positive thinking to cure themselves of diseases like cancer (see Louise Hay's story in the book *You Can Heal Your Life*). Even Holocaust survivor Viktor Frankl has written extensively about his extraordinary ability to think in philosophical and positive ways despite witnessing some of the most horrific travesties against humankind. His book *Man's*

Search for Meaning was originally published in 1946, and over the course of his life he developed many Positive Psychology theories, including Dereflection and Attitude Modification. Ultimately, these inspirational souls put their faith in a higher power to maintain their sense of trust and optimism, and all of humanity can also take guidance in realising their wider life purpose.

Transcend the Ego State

For many people, negative thoughts, energies, and life events simply come from being trapped in the ego state. Buddhism, in particular, asserts that once an individual is able to transcend ego through non-attachment, then pain and suffering will no longer be part of their reality. Many people can see the value of having an Earth-bound human experience, in which the full array of life occurrences leads to deep insight and wisdom (this often means learning to survive highly difficult times of struggle, hardship, sorrow, grief, and depression). Nonetheless, it is always possible to move beyond personal ego and detach from the state of suffering whenever desired. By feeling humility and gratitude in the face of challenging life events, as well as a consistent form of optimism and positive emotions (like joy and appreciation), the mind can stay calm and find better ways to cope with tough or tragic times (thereby minimising the ego's attachment to suffering). Being able to transcend ego and enter into a more accepting, philosophical, and objective state can save a great deal of time and energy-consuming mental angst. This skill is especially useful for those who wish to stay focused on higher justice causes, rather than perpetually reacting to any low-level dramas that may be emerging in daily life.

Rapidly rising above petty issues also generates attraction of more like-minded people who are dedicated to similar noble causes, as well as increased opportunities to realise world improvement goals. Transcending the ego state, then, is a very effective method for letting go of negative mental processes and associated life stresses, thereby creating a more ideal disposition for generating positive world change.

Engage in Deep Reflection Then Focus on the Present

Reflection involves intense mental activity: interpreting past behaviours and events; analysing patterns that have occurred throughout one's life; making judgements and evaluations about important experiences; and consciously deciding how to engage in transformation to generate a preferred future. Active involvement with one's own thoughts is an extremely important dimension of reflection, however, rather than reacting to any associated emotions in a loud, overt, or destructive way, it is important to respond to them calmly, quietly, and rationally. After thoroughly processing (or working through) the past in an objective way, it is then easier to properly leave it behind (through a sense of closure), and find greater joy in the present.

Much of Buddhist and Taoist philosophy focuses on the notion of living in the present as a path to mindfulness, a greater spiritual reality, and transcendence itself. Many New Age writers have also written extensively about the value of fully engaging with the present moment as a path to true consciousness and mental peace (that is, connecting with the here and now rather than constantly living in the past or being preoccupied with worry about a not-yet-existent future).

In terms of personal empowerment, then, individuals focused on what action they can take in the present (and how they can productively transmute the pain they are carrying from the past) are undoubtedly better able to bring positive change to the wider world.

Make Moving Forward the End Goal

Signs that an individual has successfully moved on from a period of excess negative mental energy include that they are able to:
- view the realities of their life situation in a philosophical way;
- readily give up self-destructive activities and behaviours;
- remove themselves from harmful external environments;
- enthusiastically welcome change and new opportunities;
- let those who are not interested in relationships of mutual respect move out of their life;
- allow their heart to be open to broader humanity; and
- be confident in the knowledge that they can be happy and successful in creating globally beneficial change in this lifetime.

In this open and positive state, an individual is then significantly more empowered in terms of being able to achieve their life mission of crafting a preferable world reality.

Be Open-Minded and Non-Judgemental

A large amount of negative human thought is generated from closed- or narrow-minded thinking and judgemental or prejudicial attitudes. The process of envisioning multiple future possibilities encourages opening of the mind and assists with realisation that life is a blank canvas simply waiting for the individual to make their own unique mark on it. Instead of mourning the end of a significant life phase, it is possible to see it as a time of new opportunity that allows the space for a complete reimagining of all that is to come (including many periods of excitement and joy). It is also important to move into a more empowered frame of mind in order to actively and easily make key changes. The completion of any life cycle is an excellent time to review all those aspects of one's daily reality that no longer provide satisfaction, spiritual fulfilment, or enjoyment. Inviting new energies can be achieved by making a series of small changes in each life area, or by opting for big and radical alterations (like pursuing a new career or moving overseas). The ability to effectively clear stale energies that no longer serve any beneficial life purpose can then generate a sense of new beginnings, with fresh opportunities arriving soon after.

As well, humans are more inclined to comprehend the notions of unity and to think about other peoples in positive ways by:
- being curious about all aspects of the world;
- expanding the mind through engagement in lifelong learning;
- working to understand divergent ideologies and challenging theories;
- staying open to new ideas, multiple styles of thinking, and alternative worldviews; and
- balancing critical analysis with non-judgement.

Taking an active interest in diverse cultures; listening to the life stories of many different kinds of people; and engaging with artefacts from a range of sources (be it music, film, literature, dance, or art) can also lead to great open-mindedness and positive forms of acceptance, understanding, and tolerance - all key for generating world change that results in greater forms of harmony.

CHAPTER 11
EMOTIONAL WELL-BEING ACTIVITIES

Life stress can be greatly minimised by learning valuable lessons from, then actively working to eliminate (or evolve beyond), any circumstances which are generating negative emotional responses. Where external alterations are not possible, it is important to learn how to deal with all situations in an emotionally healthy way. Mastering the art of emotional control can subsequently lead to an increased ability to solve everyday problems in a calm and efficient way, thus allowing more time and opportunity to also generate beneficial change at the global level. More emotionally positive individuals also have higher vibratory rates, which further equates with an enhanced personal capacity to improve the world at all levels.

Learn Relevant Lessons From Disrespectful People and Harmful Situations Then Evolve Beyond Them

For most humans, emotional drama is something that only emerges as a result of interactions with other people. While these external trials are no doubt a reflection of one's own internal emotional state (for instance, an individual may be with an abusive partner because they themselves are struggling with issues of self-worth), it is always a good idea to evaluate which particular life relationships and circumstances (such as work or a social setting) are generating positive or negative emotional responses. At all times, the aim should be to maximise connection with people who make others feel respected, valued, appreciated, and loved. Where possible, it is emotionally beneficial to rapidly learn key life lessons, then consciously move away from (or psychologically evolve beyond) individuals who work to undermine, diminish, denigrate, and sabotage fellow humans. If it is not possible to create physical distance with certain people (such as young dependents), then it is important to permanently come to a deeper or more philosophical understanding of why they are presenting key emotional challenges. For instance, it may be that they are providing reminders of traumatic childhood experiences, and there could be larger psychological or karmic reasons for such life themes reappearing.

If the feeling is that *everybody* is causing emotional distress, then it might be wise to take some time out to analyse one's own internal state of being (in other words, the real problem probably lies more with personal psychology rather than external individuals). It is also important to acknowledge that sometimes everything needs to collapse, and everybody needs to be removed, so that there can then be an exclusive focus on self-healing and the gradual reintroduction of only those friends, family members, and colleagues who are kind, respectful, and caring souls. For some people, a long period of personal 'time out' (constituting several months, years, or even decades) is an essential phase in the overall life journey so that ultimate soul purpose can be consciously discovered or clarified. As such, respectfully allowing self and others distance or space at critical junctures can be crucial for the evolution of the whole of humanity and the universe itself.

Meanwhile, making big life changes with respect to leaving toxic workplaces and social gatherings can actively generate increased levels of emotional calm and happiness. Sometimes an individual simply has to rise above the fear of not knowing what will come next, as when they do leave the old behind and create a new space, something else invariably comes to fill it – if that is not better, then at least there has been the acquisition of knowledge of how to activate change and keep moving forward into the future. Good emotional health may, indeed, come from being able to:
- let go of (or evolve beyond) negative or disrespectful people and harmful situations;
- embrace flexibility and move with the flow; and
- stay excited about who and what comes next.

Maintaining positivity and making life space also allows for the attraction of more supportive relationships and friendships that can provide better assistance on the path to enacting positive world change.

Heal Emotionally by Holding Self and Others to Account

Where difficult ongoing emotions are preventing healing and personal evolution, it may be useful to engage in a range of clearing exercises. For example, emotional resolution or closure can be sought through symbolic means. Survivors of gross mistreatment could, for instance, dream about somebody apologising to them, then offering forgiveness in return. The reverse scenario might also be effective where the guilty party is wanting to make amends with a wronged person who has passed on. Alternatively, letters or emails can be used to explore more complicated issues in a clear, carefully considered, and detailed way. It is important, however, to be psychologically prepared for the fact that no response (or no form of desired deserved reply) may be received. For some people, the mere act of writing about the issues (even without returned contact) can be enough to bring a sense of closure, so this can still be an excellent strategy for emotional healing.

If face-to-face conversation or confrontation would be best to properly resolve outstanding emotional issues, then it is important to think carefully about how another person might react. It is up to the individual to decide whether they have the emotional strength to deal with an interaction that could potentially be extremely negative in nature. For those who believe that they must at least *attempt* resolution (regardless of the consequences) in order to move forward in their life, then it is wise to proceed with awareness that there may also be a requirement to process more short-term pain. Regardless of the outcome, staying open to the experience itself can greatly enhance an understanding of one's own emotional blockages.

For those who are feeling consumed by negative emotions, it is worth remembering that all things must, and do, pass – patience and humility are key, but professional help can be very valuable when required. Some of the wide-ranging benefits of psychotherapy include assisting individuals to:
- talk out their feelings rather them suppressing them;
- forgive self and others;
- confront self-doubts;
- determine what repeatedly causes most pain;
- pay attention to, and express, inner needs; and
- examine one's emotional and relationship history.

For those committed to a path of emotional self-healing, it may be of additional use to determine all past and present souls with whom there are lingering issues, and to subsequently decide if there are patterns in the kinds of problems that are emerging. For instance, an individual may be allowing certain people to repeatedly take financial advantage of them because they feel guilty if they are not always 'generous'. Another example might be that someone is consistently leaving themselves open to frequent forms of criticism because they have low self-esteem (possibly as a result of bullying suffered as a child). There may be others who attract various forms of abuse because of some kind of deep-seated dislike or loathing of self. At this point it would be useful to analyse the symbolic or archetypal purpose of the people being attracted, and how there may be a playing out of certain emotional processes for specific psychological, karmic, or cosmic reasons. There may also be individuals who take on such Freudian roles as father, mother, son, daughter, brother, or sister (so that family and childhood emotional issues can be worked through and resolved), or archetypal roles like the rival, the knight in shining armour, the nemesis, or the hero (to assist with realisation of one's overall life purpose). Knowledge of Eastern and Western astrological types can further enhance understanding of the different life roles that people play, and the way that emotional dramas manifest. For instance, a Fire sign who has been in love with a Water sign may have found that all their hopes for the relationship were quickly 'extinguished' (because water is used to put out fire) and, as such, they may consciously move to spending more time with Air signs (who 'breathe life' into fire) as a way to feel more supported. An Earth sign, meanwhile, may find that they become too 'hardened' in the course of a relationship with a Fire sign (who elicits conflict through confrontational interactions), so the next partner they choose is a Water sign who will help them to 'soften' emotionally.

As well, if not just life, but relationships themselves are seen as a journey (rather than a final destination), then it is possible to understand that all connections have a set duration and, once the relevant parties have had key experiences, they will inevitably come to a close. Knowing that all interactions have their own natural energy beginnings and endings can also help people to appreciate the transient nature of their time with other human beings. If relationships are thought of as learning opportunities – where individuals are taken to many highs and lows to help them gain a greater insight into the human condition – then they will be more open to letting go when no new knowledge is able to be sourced from a partnership. Perceiving other people as mere 'destinations' or 'labels' is extremely limiting where notions of evolving energies are concerned, and connections which have passed their 'use-by' date are a significant cause of stunted spiritual growth. Even when there is resistance to a relationship ending, it may still be possible to recognise how, ultimately, one will be better off for having completed a set journey so that a more interesting and rewarding future partnership can be enjoyed.

Whatever emotions an individual may be confronting or grappling with, the process of healing can often be cyclical, lifelong / ongoing, and most effective when both the self (for attracting emotional drama) and others (for causing pain) are held to account. Consistently clearing negative emotions and understanding their role in the greater life journey or scheme of existence can then make people better equipped to transform the world in positive ways.

Clear Deep Trauma, Multiple Levels of Emotional Pain, and Problematic Patterns

Clearing one level of pain can further show how it is possible to let go of deeper trauma, or, alternatively, compounding all past and present dramas can help identify patterns and a common psychological strategy to resolve multiple issues simultaneously. Often in life, people are provided with follow-up situations which serve as a miniaturised version, or an 'echo', of previous difficulties. The way an individual deals with those subsequent challenges can provide deeper insight into how recurring problems are able to be permanently eliminated. New or more considered responses can also serve as a reinforcement of the key lessons that have been learnt whilst working through larger dramas. As well, individuals can be presented with smaller parallel scenarios (which are either easier *or* more difficult) in order to establish how well they are able to emotionally cope with working through patterns whenever they re-emerge. Given that Freudian and Jungian psychology rest on the notion that individuation (realisation of the self or 'psychic wholeness') can be achieved when personal (often childhood) traumas are consciously recognised and integrated into the psyche, it makes sense that a human soul will be given multiple chances over the course of their life to resolve them. The appearance of opportunities to consciously realise and address (or psychologically come to terms with) major life themes may be cyclical or occur in an upward spiralling fashion throughout an individual's lifetime (or even across multiple lives). Where successful psychic integration of a drama (or, more specifically, a healthy emotional response to it) has occurred, then it may be that the 'echo' is actually a real-life model of how a problematic situation is now able to resolve itself without any additional action on behalf of the individual (trusting in the ability of the universe to work as a co-creator in eliminating recurring traumas may also be a wise choice).

Furthermore, the concept of cosmic patterns may mean that when one member of a soul tribe evolves to greater psychological awareness and emotional freedom, then all members of that tribe can (or will) learn the lesson in a highly rapid and efficient manner (that is, with a massively reduced amount of pain and fuss). Soul tribe members may be able to actively help each other take 'short-cuts' in transcending recurring parallel dramas, otherwise rapid global change may occur through a process of morphic resonance. This latter concept was developed by biochemist Rupert Sheldrake and claims that self-organising systems can inherit a memory from other similar systems, or, according to the '100th monkey theory', when a certain number of monkeys [or humans] learn a new behaviour, many monkeys [or humans] can then simultaneously (or almost simultaneously) exhibit that same behaviour - regardless of whether they are in completely different time zones or world locations. According to such theories, the spiritual evolution of humanity can be significantly hastened and advanced by individuals consciously working to integrate the emotions associated with central life traumas into their psyches, and subsequently experiencing greater emotional freedom, personal happiness, wholeness, positivity, and an increased vibratory rate (which then enables enhanced abilities to create a better world).

Objectively Respond to Life Challenges

A common recommendation for people who are allowing extreme emotions to control their behaviours and lives is that they should learn how to objectively respond (not automatically negatively react) to their life circumstances. One way that this can be done is by seeing life as a play with a number of 'Acts' in which everybody is merely performing a role. By impersonally looking at life as a larger cosmic drama (in which everyone is just playing a small part), it is possible to become more of an observer of how things are unfolding for a greater purpose. As such, there is no need to emotionally over-react to every minor issue that presents itself. One can stay focused on the fact that there is a much bigger picture being formed and, however difficult what is happening may seem, ultimately it is all a crucial part of a wider story.

Another highly effective way to cope with the emotional trials and tribulations that have to be faced in a lifetime is to see the self as a hero on a particularly interesting and entertaining journey. Encoding personal experiences as mere challenges to conquer on the heroic path allows the individual to perceive all difficulties in an objective way. Suddenly a tragedy that seemed insurmountable can be reinterpreted as simply another life obstacle that is able to be actively confronted and overcome. Many people can emotionally handle setbacks when they understand that they are only temporary in nature - 'failures' frequently being used to strengthen one's resolve to work or try harder in the future, thereby spurring the individual on to even greater heights. When people are able to convince themselves that they can successfully deal with small life trials, then it is also possible to develop a self-perception as a strong superhero who is capable of fearlessly solving all major emotional problems.

As well, age and life experience can, for many, be key to becoming more efficient at recognising and processing difficult emotions. For some, the settling of hormones can lead to emotional maturity, while for others the ongoing repetition of certain life patterns can result in a kind of victim mentality, in which they continue to be plagued by extremely negative emotions (regardless of the number of years they have been on the planet). At any point, taking a 'bird's-eye view' of one's whole life (and the historical events that led to current circumstances) can allow the individual to see what exactly they have survived, and those strategies which they have been able to develop and employ to best cope with a range of emotional challenges. Many psychologists agree that resilient people who see themselves as survivors are better able to quickly move beyond any complex dramas that may emerge, and subsequently return to a state of emotional equilibrium and well-being. While there is a legitimate concern that many spiritually-oriented people simply bypass difficult dramas (such as by meditating themselves into a 'blissed out' state), it is also important to recognise that once key emotional challenges have been properly and successfully worked through, then individuals should be able to deal with all future personal issues in a quicker and more efficient way. By liberating the emotional self, a person can then devote more time to their wider life purpose, including focusing on social justice and environmental causes that are of global importance. Ultimately, learning how to be emotionally literate, emotionally intelligent, and emotionally disciplined can all be crucial in terms of how well an individual is able to respond to life difficulties, and how rapidly they are able to enter into a positive, stress-free state that allows them to better work on generating a preferable world reality.

Appreciate Nature's Cycles as a Path to Emotional Healing

Another way to engage in acts of emotional healing is by appreciating the symbolic dimension of various natural cycles. As with the four seasons recognised by Western cultures, Penney Peirce notes in *The Intuitive Way* that life also has periods of new growth (Spring); ripening (Summer); shedding (Autumn); and hibernation (Winter). As exciting as new growth and satisfying as ripening are, shedding and hibernation are also extremely important phases in the natural cycle, and people must learn to embrace them wholeheartedly and without resistance. A period of 'time out' (hibernation) is a crucial phase for resting, reflecting, healing, and growing in wisdom. Nature can provide a further model for how to be resilient in the face of adversity: how to weather a storm; survive a long dry spell; go with the flow of a strong current; or produce new shoots after a fire. According to Peirce, by connecting with nature, humans can understand that the entirety of life is, itself, a creative process that moves through a number of cycles. As such, it is important to trust endings and beginnings, as these represent the soul changing direction (in a state of calm, it is possible to flow in and out of transitional phases without getting stuck in emotions like fear or resistance).

Similarly, for the Indigenous Noongar peoples of Western Australia, nature's seasons are deeply symbolic of the cycle of life (including birth, youth, and fertility). Their six seasons cannot be rigidly defined according to artificially assigned months on a calendar (as Westerners have come to do), but they more flexibly start and end in accordance with changes in temperature, weather, flora, and fauna activity. Humans can learn many important emotional lessons from conceptualising the seasons as the Noongar do, including that flexibility is essential for survival, and that different phases of the life journey are of variable duration. Renewal is a constant process, and everything (good and bad) will come to pass. Ultimately, the cyclical nature of life (birth, death, rebirth) and the seasons, as well as the notion of 'going with the flow', can all be used in the personal development of greater emotional strength (an essential quality for withstanding any demanding processes that accompany being an active agent of extensive world change).

Engage in Random Acts of Kindness or Become a Volunteer

In line with the philosophy of helping others to promote emotional healing of self is the phenomenon of engaging in regular or random acts of kindness. The 'pay it forward' concept provides a good example of how doing one act of kindness for another can then multiply down the line, with the ultimate goal being to have entire societies dedicated to acts of selflessness rather than greed and mistreatment of others. On a karmic level, helping, caring for, or being kind to others is also energetically desirable. While an individual should not over-help (and thus disempower) those in their immediate life who may treat the relationship like it is a 'one way street', it is nonetheless possible to regularly assist the truly needy, complete strangers, or the environment itself (including local wildlife) without developing a growing sense of resentment or anger. Regularly completing a random act of kindness can make the world a more positive place on a vibrational level, as well as enhance self-esteem; make a person feel more spiritually and emotionally fulfilled; and create a deeper sense of life happiness.

Volunteer work is another way to live in accordance with the philosophy of advancing one's own emotional healing by helping (or striving to heal) others. Offering personal time and skills to serve others - without the promise of financial reward – is a humbling experience and allows an individual to realise that, at any given time, there is always somebody in the world who is experiencing more life difficulty or emotional hardship. In the act of assisting others, people are inevitably required to focus less on their own troubles and concerns, which can provide a very welcome reprieve from repetitive thoughts and emotions that are negative in character. Working to help others (in a balanced and non-draining way) can further generate many positive emotions that promote an increase in the personal vibratory rate, thereby allowing a greater capacity to create a better world.

Give Up Toxic Aspects of Western Society

In choosing to help others as a powerful kind of emotional healing, it is also worth remembering that notions of providing lifelong forms of holistic love and care have long been an essential part of traditional Indigenous cultures. Interdependence and the maintenance of harmony within small kinship clans are still a fundamental part of survival for many Indigenous peoples. By comparison, contemporary Western lifestyles are based on ideologies of selfish individualism, greed, competition, and materialism (rather than sharing, cooperation, and nurture), and are a major cause for the escalation of negative energies (including mental health and emotional problems). Thus, by engaging in regular acts of kindness and giving up limiting and toxic aspects of Western society, humanity can become stronger, more emotionally whole, and much better able to improve the world at the wider level.

Develop an Attitude of Gratitude

Shedding tears is a normal and natural way of clearing negative emotions (it is the body's means of providing physical relief through the release of healing chemicals), however after large amounts of weeping following any emotional tribulation, it is important to think deeply about all personal life aspects which are good or positive in nature. Putting personal experiences into proper perspective on a global scale (that is, in a world where literally billions of people are suffering from starvation, crippling poverty, or political oppression) helps individuals realise how important it is to develop an attitude of gratitude for even those seemingly simple things that so many daily take for granted: clean water, fresh food, shelter, and spare change. Being grateful for all life blessings can not only help an individual let go of past issues in a more accepting, gracious, and complete way, but also provide strength and inspiration to move beyond current emotional dramas and guilt complexes, and work to help those who are far less fortunate in this lifetime. Many psychological and spiritual theories regard qualities such as humility and gratitude as being key to transcending the ego state, and thus an important precursor to being able to effectively improve the world for all of humanity.

*Additional strategies for clearing negative physical, mental, and emotional energies are featured in Appendix E.

APPENDICES

Appendix A: Insight Into the Spiritual Relationship Between Native Americans and Nature
Excerpts From Letter by Chief Seattle (Si'ahl or Seahtl)

Appendix B: Infinity as a Universal and Unifying Concept
- The Word 'Infinity' in Other Languages
- Common Cross-Cultural Meanings Equated With The Infinity Symbol
- Early Mathematical and Scientific Conceptions of Infinity

Spiritual Conceptions of Infinity
- Ancient Origins of Infinity as a Spiritual Symbol and Concept
- Hindu Conceptions of Infinity
- Buddhist Conceptions of Infinity
- Other Spiritual Conceptions of Infinity

Conceptions of Infinity in Nature-Based Spiritual Beliefs
- Forms of Nature Worship
- Traditional Indigenous Conceptions of Infinity
- Celtic Pagan Conceptions of Infinity
- Shinto Conceptions of Infinity
- Taoist Conceptions of Infinity

Other Nature-Based Conceptions of Infinity
- The Gaia Concept
- The Sacred Balance
- Connecting to Infinity Through Nature
- The Benefits of Developing a Conception of Infinity

Appendix C: Dietary Guidelines
- Fruit and Vegetables
- Grain (Cereal) Foods
- Lean Meat and Alternatives
- Milk, Yoghurt, Cheese, and / or Alternatives
- Unsaturated Spreads and Oils

Appendix D: The Physical, Psychological, and Social Effects of Substance Use and Abuse

Appendix E: Strategies for Clearing Negative Energies

APPENDIX A
INSIGHT INTO THE SPIRITUAL RELATIONSHIP BETWEEN NATIVE AMERICANS AND NATURE

In an 1854 speech, Suquamish and Duwamish (Native American) Chief Seattle (Si'ahl or Seahtl) responds to the government's offer to purchase tribal land by repeatedly questioning the spiritually disconnected and extremely environmentally destructive actions of Westerners. He identifies several problematic Western behaviours, including over-population of the land; heavy technology dependency; extensive removal of flora; and widescale destruction of fauna and habitat. He begs Westerners to love and care for the land as his people have, and to preserve the land for all children. Along with the spiritual value of the land, Chief Seattle (Si'ahl or Seahtl) outlines the familial relationship between his people and all of nature.

Excerpts From Speech by Chief Seattle (Si'ahl or Seahtl)*:
"How can you buy or sell the sky, the warmth of the land? The idea is strange to us. If we do not own the freshness of the air and the sparkle of the water, how can you buy them? Every part of this earth is sacred to my people. Every shining pine needle, every sandy shore, every mist in the dark woods, every clearing and humming insect is holy in the memory and experience of my people. The sap which courses through the trees carries the memories of the red man...

We are part of the earth and it is part of us. The perfumed flowers are our sisters; the deer, the horse, the great eagle, these are our brothers. The rocky crests, the juices of the meadows, the body heat of the pony, and man – all belong to the same family...

The ashes of our fathers are sacred. Their graves are holy ground, and so these hills, these trees, this portion of earth is consecrated to us. We know that the white man does not understand our ways. One portion of land is the same to him as the next, for he is a stranger who comes in the night and takes from the land whatever he needs. The earth is not his brother, but his enemy, and when he has conquered it, he moves on. He leaves his fathers' graves behind, and he does not care. He kidnaps the earth from his children. He does not care. His fathers' graves and his children's birthright are forgotten. He treats his mother, the earth, and his brother, the sky, as things to be bought, plundered, sold like sheep or bright beads. His appetite will devour the earth and leave behind only a desert...

I have seen a thousand rotting buffaloes on the prairie, left by the white man who shot them from a passing train. I am a savage and I do not understand how the smoking iron horse can be more important than the buffalo that we kill only to stay alive...

What is man without the beasts? If all the beasts were gone, men would die from great loneliness of spirit. For whatever happens to the beasts, soon happens to man. All things are interconnected...

You must teach your children that the ground beneath their feet is the ashes of our grandfathers. So that they will respect the land, tell your children that the earth is rich with the lives of our kin. Teach your children what we have taught our children - that the earth is our mother. Whatever befalls the earth befalls the sons of the earth. If men spit upon the ground, they spit upon themselves...

Where is the thicket? Gone. Where is the eagle? Gone. And what is it to say goodbye to the swift pony and the hunt? The end of living and the beginning of survival. This we know. The earth does not belong to man; man belongs to the earth. This we know. All things are connected like the blood which unites one family. All things are connected. Whatever befalls the earth befalls the sons of the earth. Man did not weave the web of life; he is merely a strand in it. Whatever he does to the web, he does to himself... The whites too shall pass; perhaps sooner than all other tribes. Continue to contaminate your bed, and you will one night suffocate in your own waste...

When the last red man has vanished from this earth, and his memory is only the shadow of a cloud moving across the prairie, these shores and forests will still hold the spirits of my people. For they love this earth as the newborn loves its mother's heartbeat. So, if we sell you our land, love it as we've loved it. Care for it as we've cared for it. Hold in your mind the memory of the land as it is when you take it. And with all your strength, with all your mind, with all your heart, preserve it for your children and love it."

*Due to the later translation of this speech from Duwamish (by H. A. Smith in 1887), there are now some disputes about the accuracy of the wording. These excerpts rely on the Smith version and have been sourced from: Suzuki, David (1990) *Inventing the Future: Reflections on Science, Technology, and Nature*. Toronto: Stoddart.

APPENDIX B
INFINITY AS A UNIVERSAL AND UNIFYING CONCEPT

The word 'Infinity' appears in multiple languages, disciplines, and spiritual beliefs, suggesting that it is a universal (and, thus, potentially unifying) concept. This Appendix provides additional insight into the Infinity concept as it is conceived in a wide range of cultures and faiths. Proponents of creating a better world can potentially harness the power of The Infinite to generate positive change, or they can use the cross-cultural and multidisciplinary nature of the idea to unify diverse peoples (thereby bringing greater harmony to social relations on a global scale).

The Word 'Infinity' in Other Languages
There is much evidence to suggest that Infinity is a universal concept. The following equivalent words - sourced from a wide range of global languages and cultures - supports this theory.

African
Afrikaans: oneindig; Chichewa: osawerengeka; Hausa: rashin iyaka; Igbo: ebighebi; Kinyarwanda: ubuziraherezo; Sesotho: egoist; Shona: kusaguma; Somali: xad la'aan; Xhosa: ngokungapheliyo; Swahili, Yoruba, and Zulu: infinity.

Asian
Albanian: sonsuzluq; Chinese: wuqiong; Georgian, Hmong, and Khmer: infinity; Turkish: caksizlik; and Uzbek: cheksizlik.

Austronesian
Cebuano and Malagasy: infinity; Filipino: kawalang-hanggan; Hawaiian: palena pau 'ole; Indonesian: tak terbatas; Javanese: pandjenengan; Malay: infiniti; Māori: mutu; Samoan: le iu; and Sundanese: takterhingga.

European
Albanian and Catalan: infinit; Basque: infinitua; Bosnian and Croatian: beskraj; Corsican: infinitu; Czech and Slovak: nekonecno; Danish: uendelighed; Dutch: oneindigheid; Estonian: lopmatus; Finnish: aarettomyys; French: infini; Frisian: uneinigens; Galician, Italian, and Spanish: infinito; German: Unendlichkeit; Greek: apeiro; Hungarian: vegtelenseg; Icelandic: oendanlegt; Irish and Scots Gaelic:

Infinity; Latvian: bezgaliba; Lithuanian: begalybe; Luxembourgish: onendlechkeet; Maltese: infinita; Norwegian: evighet; Polish: nieskonczonosc; Portuguese: infinidade; Russian: beskonechnost; Swedish: oandlighet; Ukrainian: neskinchennist; Welsh: anfeidredd.

Others
Arabic: ma la nihaya; Esperanto: senfineco; and Latin: infinitum.

*There are many other examples of the word 'Infinity' in languages that use non-alphabetical script - please refer to the *In Different Languages* website for a list of these.

Common Cross-Cultural Meanings Equated With The Infinity Symbol (∞)

1. The Infinity symbol (∞) can be seen as a never-ending double loop, representing the cyclic and infinite nature of the universe, energy, the human soul, and spirit. This includes the endless cycle of all life (continuous creation); death (destruction); and rebirth (resurrection, renewal, or regeneration). Just as the Infinity sign goes 'round and round', so too is everything (all energy) fluid and a part of the everlasting circle. As such, the Infinity symbol can represent:
   - the mysticism of the past;
   - a present link to eternity;
   - the boundless potential of a limitless future; and
   - ongoing spiritual development through growing awareness of these multiple levels of reality.
2. The Infinity symbol (∞) can be viewed as two equal parts that are connected and can never be separated: one part simply cannot exist without the other. On a symbolic level, such inseparability makes an Infinity connection unbreakable - an indestructible, unstoppable, and everlasting force.
3. The two sections of the Infinity symbol (∞) can be understood as representing two eternally interlinked - or interlocking or intermeshed - individuals or elements (such as Yin and Yang). Where dualism and opposition exist on the Earth plane (such as in the form of 'dark' and 'light'), unity and equilibrium exist in Infinity: two equally balanced forces together become one.

Some common forms of the Infinity symbol (∞) include:

1. Celtic Knot (also known as an Endless Knot or Mystic Knot): Intricate knots interweave and overlap to signify no beginning and no end (an infinite or never-ending loop).
2. Swedish Malin Symbol (an Infinity symbol with an arrow breaking the centre): An individual must experience setbacks and challenges in order to grow (psychologically and spiritually).
3. Double Infinity (two Infinity signs intertwined - also known as an Infinity x Infinity or an Infinity + Infinity sign): Implies harmony, beauty, balance, equilibrium, and perfection; double absoluteness; or eternal commitments coming together (the intertwined forms representing shared karmic responsibilities).
4. Infinity Names and Infinity Heart (a heart with an Infinity sign through it, or two heart shapes connected like an Infinity symbol): Two names placed on the Infinity sign symbolises togetherness, as well as an eternal bond between partners, relatives, or friends. The heart shapes represent limitless love or an eternal connection.

In the world of love (romantic, platonic, familial), the Infinity symbol (∞) is very popular and is regularly used in the form of jewellery as a gift between people who feel deeply connected (lovers, friends, relatives). The adjoined sides of the Infinity sign can represent two people coming together in a relationship and being spiritually attached for eternity. An Infinity connection holds the promise of:
- true love;
- loyalty;
- being together forever;
- becoming as one;
- love that stands the test of time;
- a love that holds no bounds (for better or worse);
- eternal love (or love without an end); and
- spiritual love.

Notions of The Infinite are also evoked via such ideas as that love brings limitless possibilities, and that unconditional love is boundless (completely without judgement and everlasting in nature). Where the nature of love is to be Infinite, then emotions like jealousy and fear come to hold no sway. Love itself as a path to Infinity is also embodied in the phrase, "To see Infinity, love first." Potentially, then, the reader could eclipse all other suggested paths to Infinity by simply filling their heart with overwhelming, unconditional love for self; every person in their immediate sphere; all of humanity; and nature as a whole. Ultimately, the Infinity symbol (∞) is a reminder that there is endless love and energy in the universe.

Other common understandings and uses associated with the Infinity symbol (∞) are outlined below.

- The appearance of the Infinity symbol (∞) can often signify an upcoming truce or reconciliation (a reconnection of two sides).
- Practitioners of meditation frequently focus on the Infinity symbol (∞) as a way to gain clarity and manifest healing.
- For those who draw a numerological connection between the Infinity symbol and the number 8 (∞ being a sideways 8), there is the belief that '808' represents The Infinity State. In many religious contexts, 8 is also regarded as the number of the initiate (relating to having previously passed through seven phases of spiritual growth).

Early Mathematical and Scientific Conceptions of Infinity

Evidence suggests that Infinity as a mathematical concept was first developed by Greek philosopher Zeno (circa 495-430 BCE). In the 4th-3rd centuries BCE, Ancient Indian (Jain) mathematicians also classified numbers into sets: enumerable, innumerable, and infinite. These mathematicians noted two types of infinite numbers:

- Asaṃkhyāta – countless / innumerable; and
- Ananta – endless / unlimited.

Contemporary mathematicians continue to use Infinity to describe the cardinality of a set that does not have a finite number of elements (in set theory, numbers go on forever - there are infinite real numbers). For mathematicians, the Infinity sign can also represent a potential (rather than actual) infinite quantity.

Meanwhile, the first published theory of a limitless universe was attributed to Englishman Thomas Digges in 1576, but the Infinity symbol itself did not appear until the following century. In 1655, chief cryptographer for the British Parliament, John Wallis, used $1/\infty$ as a notation indicating something infinitesimal, or so small that it cannot be measured. Wallis' work is credited as being one of the inspirations for the development of calculus, and a significant influence on many philosophers, scientists, and physicists (including fellow Brit Isaac Newton, who wrote about equations with infinite numbers in 1699).

Also of interest is that the lemniscate (meaning 'ribbon') was used by the Greek philosopher Proclus (around the 5th century) to describe a shape that could be imagined as a twisted ribbon that has no beginning or end. In other words, if a person were to start tracing from any point, they would never reach an end, but rather continue on a loop forever. (Proclus originally conceived the shape as two horses' hooves connected together.) The lemniscate was then made famous by mathematician James Booth in the 19th century when he developed the geometrical concept Booth's Curve (also known as the Hippopede of Proclus).

Spiritual Conceptions of Infinity

Infinity is mentioned, and holds a significant meaning, in a wide range of faiths, spiritualities, and religious beliefs. Common to most faiths is the notion that life is infinite: while an individual soul's time on Earth may be finite, spirit exists forever. Many religions also conceptualise - or actively describe - their relevant divine / deified being as Infinity itself. As well, the Infinity symbol can be regarded as having a kind of universal spiritual power. People of diverse faiths may revere the symbol and focus on it during prayer or meditation in order to experience intense revelations and significant gains in wisdom (a sense of peace and oneness being important pursuits in the realisation of spiritual growth). Where humans are often required to operate in a complicated and chaotic world, the Infinity symbol can represent simplicity, harmony, balance, unity, and the spiritual connectedness of all things.

There are many spiritual concepts and terms / phrases that can be regarded as encompassing, or equating to, Infinity or The Infinite. Spiritual practitioners also often regard Infinity as a 'state of mind' or a 'state of being'. Religious texts, New Age writings, and several quantum theories make reference to such notions as those listed below. [Please note that the following terms are often accompanied by adjectives like Higher, Great / Greater, Essential, Ultimate, Eternal, Immortal, Spiritual, Sacred, Soul, Holy, Heavenly,

Universal, Internal, Inner, Core, Being, Living, Intelligent, Loving, One, Order, Transcendent, or Enlightened (and sometimes two or three of these descriptors in combination).]
- Oneness;
- The Whole or Wholeness;
- Unity;
- The Unified Field;
- Connectedness;
- Interconnectedness;
- The Force;
- The Power;
- The Energy (Prana / Qi / Chi);
- The Self;
- The Essence;
- The Presence;
- The Intelligence;
- The Wisdom;
- The Knowing;
- The Continuity;
- The Harmony;
- The Universe;
- The Multiverse;
- Consciousness;
- Source;
- Spirit;
- Love;
- Light or The Sun;
- Grace;
- Bliss;
- Heaven, Paradise, or Nirvana; and
- The Divine (or specific omniscient and omnipotent conceptions like The Creator, Goddess, God, Brahman, and Allah, or a deified being like Buddha).

[For the sake of consistency, this Appendix predominantly utilises the term 'Infinity' or the phrase 'The Infinite' when referring to the spiritual idea that encompasses all of the above concepts. Readers can feel free to substitute in their own preferred term, phrase, or overall concept.]

Ancient Origins of Infinity as a Spiritual Symbol and Concept

The *Mind Journal* article 'Five Secrets of The Infinity Symbol' asserts that early versions of the Infinity symbol (∞) originated in Ancient Egypt in the form of the ouroboros (the earliest pictorial record of which dates to circa 1600 BCE). The Papyrus of Dama (1077-943 BCE) shows that, during coronation, pharaohs were crowned with a snake, which served as a symbolic act indicating that they had accepted the divine power within. The snake could either be depicted as 'the coiled one' (*mehet*) or 'the risen one' (*iaret*). The coiled one has continuing spiritual significance, as it is a serpent eating its own tail (the ouroboros) and indicates that humans are bound to endlessly reincarnate on the Earth plane unless they learn their lessons (these can be gained from challenging life experiences that are ultimately designed to lead to an awakening). The risen one, then, symbolises the act of awakening itself, whereby an individual begins a spiritual ascension. The Ancient Egyptians further believed that, in the course of rising up to claim its true power and engage in acts of justified defence, the snake used its light to fight against darkness – hence the notion of human spiritual awakening still being regarded as a movement into the light. Awakening ends the cycle of infinite incarnations (The Karmic Circle or The Circle of Life: Birth, Death, and Rebirth).

In Ancient India, the Yoga-Kundalini Upanishad (circa 1000-500 BCE) also described kundalini as a divine power that was like a snake coiled around upon itself, holding its tail in its mouth and lying resting half asleep at the base of the body. When awakened, this energy could then rise up the spine and out through the crown chakra, presumably reconnecting with Infinity.

The ouroboros and its link to the ideas of immortality, infinite return, and eternity was carried over millennia to peoples and cultures all around the world. For example, the Ancient Greeks adopted the ouroboros in circa 400 CE, as, subsequently, did the Ancient Romans, and it was featured widely on objects like magical talismans and emblems. The ouroboros also appeared in an alchemical text from Hellenistic Egypt, where it was represented as half black and half white – tying in with the concept of duality, where opposite forces within humans and the universe are linked (the third century BCE Chinese notion of Yin and Yang embodied this belief as well).

Another early written idea relating to Infinity dates back to Ancient Greece, when philosopher Anaximander (610–546 BCE) developed a theory of cosmology and believed the universe originated from the apeiron ('the endless'). He held that the eternal motion of time caused opposites (such as hot and cold, wet and dry, or night and day) to be separated from each other as the world came into being. He also thought that the world would one day be destroyed, back into the apeiron, to give birth to new worlds.

Hindu Conceptions of Infinity (Originating in India Circa 1500 BCE)

The main doctrine of Hinduism concerns the unity of Brahman ('God') and Atman (The Self). In *The Search for the Pearl*, Gillian Ross states that, for the Hindu, liberation (moksha) from the world's cause and effect processes, and thus fear and suffering, is achieved by the realisation that the true Self *is* Brahman. In line with many conceptions of Infinity, The Self in Hinduism is perceived as soundless, formless, intangible, and eternal (without beginning or end). In Hindu thought, knowing equates to freedom (including from death). When the individual is freed from the delusion of separateness (created by ignorance) that pervades the world of the relative (samsara), then consciousness becomes pure bliss (ananda). This kind of conscious realisation of oneness can be regarded as parallel to experiencing a deep comprehension of Infinity.

According to Hindu belief, as long as humans are caught up in samsara (believing perceptions of external 'reality' to be all there is), then they live in a state of maya (illusion), and are victims of the reactive forces of nature (karma). In this way, humans fail to experience the *true* Self (which is total freedom). Ross explains that the egoic phase of consciousness judges The Self in opposition to the world, and vice versa (that is, a belief in separateness). By dissolving the ego, the individual can see that, ultimately, nothing about their life is of any consequence and, as such, all their problems and conflicts will disappear. Thus, liberation from the karmic 'wheel of existence' requires the lifting of the 'veil of maya' and seeing the true nature of reality and The Self as divine. With such an identification, the individual becomes free of karma, because it is only attracted to the actions of personal ego. Hinduism therefore advocates self-knowledge as a path to liberation, and so focuses on the internal world of consciousness rather than the external world of the senses.

Some Hindus regard metaphysical ignorance (avidya) as at the root of all suffering, with philosophical studies then being seen as the best path to freedom. From this position, it is believed that the correct analysis of the nature of reality will help lift the 'veil of ignorance' that imprisons and tortures the soul. Other Hindus focus on devotion (bhakti yoga) as the way to liberation. According to Ross, there are also Hindus who believe that human problems are only the result of action. Since complete inaction is not, however, possible on the Earth plane, then dharma (right action) is the best means of liberation. Under this approach, all action has to be selflessly motivated by duty rather than desire, and all attachment to what is gained by action must be given up. Every branch of yoga (which is Sanskrit for 'union') further advocates a disciplined purification of mind and body (through meditation and physical actions or poses), which can allow the practitioner to enter into a state of pure consciousness. Through pranayama (or control of the life force through breath), individuals are also able to engage in sense withdrawal, meditation, and ultimately superconsciousness.

Hinduism directly acknowledges the concept of Infinity in a number of ways. The Shukarahasya Upanishad quotes the God Brahma as saying, "What is Brahman? Truth, knowledge, infinity is Brahman." This Upanishad then states that the path to liberation is via meditation using four sacred statements: "Knowledge is Brahman. I am Brahman. You are Brahman. The Atman [Self] is Brahman." For Hindus, the Infinity symbol also signifies spiritual regeneration and eternal life after death, and the number 8 (the symbol on its side) represents the initiate. An initiate is a person who has gone through the seven heavens of Hindu theology and the seven stages of spiritual enlightenment. As such, the Infinity sign is extremely important for many Hindus due to its association with resurrection and eternity.

Buddhist Conceptions of Infinity (Originating in India in the Sixth Century BCE)

Many Buddhist ideas provide a philosophical connection to notions of Infinity. According to Gillian Ross (*The Search for the*

Pearl), central to Buddhist ideology is the belief that all humans can reach Nirvana (enlightenment) by being released from desire, worldly attachments, and karmic suffering (egoic consciousness, or the illusion of the self, being the only reason people exist). Via the path of self-transformation (dharma), an individual can come to recognise that desires flow out of ignorance about the true nature of reality and the self, and it is these desires that set in motion karmic retribution and the cycle of death and rebirth. For awakening and liberation to occur, then, an individual must come to recognise and understand the transience and impermanence of everything (including the soul / ego) – not only suffering, but all life and 'reality' (including the Earth plane itself) are illusions. Ross documents how spiritual progress, or consciousness of the wisdom of 'no self' (comprehension that there is no 'I'), can be achieved through perception (right awareness) and mindfulness (right meditation), as well as feelings and acts of love, compassion, non-judgement, and equanimity (right effort and right action).

In her exploration of Buddhist philosophy, Ross also identifies many techniques for liberating consciousness from the egoic 'prison'. For example, through meditation that focuses the mind on the breath and physical sensations, an individual can deepen their awareness of energy vibration and the lack of solidity of the body (the meaninglessness of any sense of permanent self as a 'body' can therefore be experienced). During the state of meditation, the boundaries between consciousness and unconsciousness can also begin to dissolve, thereby leading to a knowing that all sensations (including physical pain) will pass. A 'this too shall pass' mentality can further manifest to psychologically evaluate all life adversity. In other words, an individual will no longer feel the need to feed egoic consciousness and karmic reactions by constantly getting caught up in problems, as everything that happens is really 'nothing'. As such, serenity can be an effective path to spiritual awareness. Many Buddhists also regard the temporary creation of mandalas using coloured sands (that can then be swept away upon completion) as a powerfully symbolic example of soul impermanence.

The idea of Alaya Consciousness provides a further way for humanity to comprehend conceptions of Infinity. The Sanskrit word 'alaya' means 'unending' or 'without limit'. For Buddhists, then, the notion of Alaya Consciousness refers to 'unending information' or 'limitless consciousness'. According to Sandra Anne Taylor

(*The Akashic Records*), consciousness is a dynamic and ever-expanding field of information. As an extension of this, she claims that Alaya Consciousness both encompasses, and is contained within, everything in the universe. Taylor further argues that all humans have a spiritual self that lives forever. Thus, as each soul's experience grows and expands, eternal consciousness also evolves.

Other Spiritual Conceptions of Infinity

This book primarily focuses on New Age, Indigenous, and Eastern ideas (due to the author's personal interests), but readers should take the initiative to investigate other spiritual conceptions and representations of Infinity as a potential way to unify many different philosophies and faiths. For example, Scientologists refer to the eighth dynamic, which is the desire for an eternal and infinite existence. Monotheistic religions like Judaism, Islam, and Christianity (and their myriad denominations) all speak of Infinity (or parallel or connected ideas) in their sacred texts and scriptures. As well, the Infinity Cross is worn by many Christians as a statement of faith or belief in God; an eternal promise to Christianity itself; and a symbolic representation of Christ's everlasting love (which grants humanity immortality).

Spiritualism, meanwhile, was originally conceived of by Emmanuel Swedenborg (in 1700s Sweden), then founded as a modern movement in 1840s New York. It rests on the belief that spirits of the dead have the ability to communicate with living souls (that is, those still residing on the Earth plane). In France in the 1850s, Allan Kardec further developed this idea into the contemporary branch of Spiritism, which places greater emphasis on reincarnation. Spiritualists see the afterlife (or The Spirit World) as a place in which passed over souls continue to evolve. Since spirits have greater knowledge, insight, and wisdom than humans, Spiritualists believe that the former are capable of providing the latter with useful information about a wide range of practical, moral, and ethical issues (as well as about the nature of Infinity itself). Spiritualists also maintain that each individual has specific spirit guides who can be consulted to provide insight at any time, regarding any matter. In this way, Spiritualism and Spiritism are faiths that provide for immediate access to Infinity for the most meaningful, current, relevant, and helpful messages.

Conceptions of Infinity in Nature-Based Spiritual Beliefs
Forms of Nature Worship

In the spiritual or religious practices of Nature Worship, individuals feel deeply connected to, and reverent of, various aspects of the natural world. For instance, practitioners of this form of worship may regard nature spirits as being responsible for specific natural locations and phenomena (like a mountain or the oceanic tides), as well as the cosmos as a whole (this provides an important link to the concept of Infinity). Nature Worship can take many different forms, including:

Animism - all parts of nature (animals, plants, rocks) are believed to be imbued with a spiritual essence;

Totemism - a sacred object or creature from nature (totem) works as an emblem of a family group, clan, or tribe;

Naturalistic Pantheism - the divine is seen to be a unified form of all natural phenomena; and

Panentheism – the divine is thought to be an integral component of every aspect of the universe, and to extend beyond space and time (this is also fundamental to many conceptions of Infinity).

Traditional Indigenous Conceptions of Infinity (Originating in Various Ancient World Cultures)

In *Native Wisdom for White Minds*, Anne Wilson Schaef explores Indigenous conceptions of nature as a means via which humanity can learn everything they need to know about self and the universe. She says that Indigenous peoples see nature as a way to gain deep spiritual wisdom, because connection with it leads to an understanding of the interconnectedness of all things, as well as balance and living in harmony with the environment (their focus is always on moving towards The Whole, or Infinity). Wilson Schaef further points out that humans can learn all their spiritual lessons in nature, because they come to understand that they are a fundamental *part* of it (a participant in it, not a controlling force above it), and they therefore live by the same laws as all of nature. She posits the argument that without nature, humans are essentially displaced, and that by actually being in natural environments (such as by walking along the coast near vast oceans, or by sleeping under the stars and endless skies) people can comprehend that they are only a small part of a much larger reality.

The Indigenous worldview also revolves around the notion that when humans care for nature, nature cares for them. This is due to the pantheistic philosophy that the divine is in all parts of nature (creeks, grasses, insects), and that a bond exists between all living things because they live on the same soil, drink the same water, and breathe the same air. The land itself is seen as the foundation of life and is therefore sacred. For nomadic gatherer-hunters (which humans have been for the majority of existence), the concept of land 'ownership' is an alien notion. Instead, they believe that people are *owned by* the land, and that they have a responsibility to take care of it (both the land and its creatures have to be respected and protected, and this is the basis of Indigenous law). For traditional Indigenous peoples, sustainability is realised through only taking from the land as much as is needed at any given time (thereby leaving something for neighbouring populations and future generations). Where belief centres on the idea that land use is granted by a greater power, it ensures the earth is viewed as sacred and that, if abused, all life will disappear. Many Indigenous peoples thus regard themselves as a steward for The Great Spirit.

These philosophies link back to the notion of the oneness of all things, and the fact that humans are always participating in a universe that is acting in partnership with them. In other words, people of the world are one, as they belong to a planet that lives and breathes as a single organism (thus when any part of the interconnected whole is damaged, everybody is affected). For traditional Indigenous peoples, higher spiritual consciousness is always accessible through oneness with nature. Schaef explains that body and spirit are united, and all forms in the land (both animate and inanimate) represent a link to the eternal. Many Polynesian peoples also emphasise love for everyone and everything (aloha in Hawai'i) and loving all people equally (aroha for the Māori of New Zealand). Indigenous peoples believe that feelings of connectedness and oneness can provide a path to spiritual and emotional healing for *all* humanity. [*See Appendix A for excerpts from an 1800s speech which provides detailed insight into the spiritual relationship that traditional Native Americans have with nature.]

Celtic Pagan Conceptions of Infinity (Originating in Western Europe Circa 500 BCE)

Celtic Pagans believe that all aspects of the natural world contain spirits, and that communication with them is possible. The Ancient Irish swore their oaths by The Three Realms (Land, Sea, and Sky), and contemporary Celtic Pagans now recognise Fire as the central inspirational force that unites the realms. Divination and other nature-bound customs, such as taking omens from the shapes of clouds or the behaviour of birds and animals, are also favoured practices of Celtic Pagans. The 'unity of all' Pagan philosophy connects deeply to the concept of Infinity, and explains how it is possible to access wisdom from Infinity via real-world signs (including natural phenomena like rain and lightning).

Shinto Conceptions of Infinity (Originating in Japan in the Sixth Century BCE)

Shinto is a polytheistic religion from Japan which involves the worship of many deities (or spirits) known as kami, and which also views natural phenomena as being divine. Shinto practitioners believe that kami are present everywhere (in a formless and invisible way), and are thus essentially infinite in number: inhabiting all organic and inorganic matter; natural events (like earthquakes and floods); natural forces (such as the wind and sunshine); and important features of the landscape (like a waterfall or rock formation). Shintoism's belief in there being a spiritual dimension to an ever-present and all-inclusive force is parallel to the notion of Infinity.

Taoist Conceptions of Infinity (Originating in China in the Sixth Century BCE)

Developed by Lao Tzu, Taoism advocates living in accordance with the way nature operates (rather than merely worshipping it), and features many philosophies that tie in with notions of Infinity. The Tao (The Way) is a concept that is all-encompassing: it covers truth, every kind of process, and is believed to run through everything (from nature to the human psyche to social relations). In other words, The Tao resides in all things, produces all things, and enables all things to exist – it is the eternal harmony of all things in all times and places. In his *Guide to Eastern Philosophy*, Jay Stevenson says that while The Tao itself never actually changes, the way it manifests itself in the world is as constant change (life and all in it is transient). According to the concept of fu, however, all things can only change to the point where they must be able to balance themselves out. In other words, things must always return from a state of extremes to a state of balance (or equilibrium). Connected to this notion of continual change and balancing out are the concepts of Yin and Yang, which are opposed, yet complementary forces that are perpetually at work in natural and human events (they represent dark and light, negative and positive, passive and active, and so on). Where there is duality (between male and female, for instance), there is also the opportunity for unity.

Ultimately, the aim of Taoism is to observe how The Tao works in nature, then to bring one's own actions into harmony with it. By balancing energies and moving consciousness back into the whole of creation, it is possible to rediscover The Tao. To achieve a Tao-tuned consciousness, then, Stevenson explains that it is important to let go of desire (which is the root of disharmony and suffering), and to embrace humility, compassion, non-violence, non-materialism, and unconditional love. From Taoist philosophical thought come the following beliefs that promote deeper understandings of Infinity: 'The Tao is bottomless. Like the source of all things. It blunts edges that are sharp. It unties tangled things. It softens all light. It unites the world into a whole. It is like dark, deep water that exists forever.'

Other Nature-Based Conceptions of Infinity
The Gaia Concept

James Lovelock's personification of Earth as Gaia (a Greek maternal goddess), or a 'living planet', has been extremely influential in terms of Westerners reconceptualising their place in the overall scheme of existence. When Earth is regarded as a single living whole, it is possible to comprehend how crucial the diversity of all life (from individual organisms to entire ecosystems) truly is. Thus, rather than regarding the primary goal of humans as being to dominate nature (a 'Man vs Nature' kind of mentality), the Gaia philosophy repositions people as just one small part of a complex living organism. Even if humans over-populate the planet or damage nature to the point that they themselves can no longer survive, Earth itself as a self-regenerating organism will recover after their extinction, and continue to live, rejuvenate, and flourish.

By perceiving the planet as a creative and nurturing force (rather than a 'resource' to be exploited and profited from), humans can come to see Earth as a single integrated whole – this is deeply relevant, in a wider sense, to the greater concept of Infinity. Photos from space also support the idea of the planet as one entity (without artificially constructed borders) in which life can only exist if certain atmospheric conditions are maintained. By revitalising traditional Indigenous conceptions of humanity's relationship with nature, the human race has a chance of surviving self-annihilation. In other words, individuals must respect, live in harmony with, and fulfil certain responsibilities to the environment in order to counter the current trends of widespread ecological devastation, resource depletion, pollution, and climate change (which scientists widely agree are caused by unsustainable growth and rampant consumption). Ultimately, Gaia dictates that it is up to people to live in accordance with the greater needs of the natural world (not the reverse). [*James Lovelock has written multiple papers and books exploring the Gaia philosophy. His earliest conception of Gaia dates back to the 1960s, and in 1979 he published *Gaia: A New Look at Life on Earth.* In more recent years he has released such titles as *Homage to Gaia*; *The Revenge of Gaia*; *The Vanishing Face of Gaia*; and *We Belong to Gaia* (amongst many others).]

The Sacred Balance

Like James Lovelock, David Suzuki provides a scientific yet deeply spiritual understanding of the relationship between humans and nature in his masterpiece *The Sacred Balance: Rediscovering Our Place in Nature.* Suzuki notes that in an interdependent universe, human beings have a great level of responsibility. Indeed, whether they are aware of it or not, each individual is accountable for the far-extending repercussions of their actions. Since past, present, and future form a continuum, each generation inherits the environmental consequences of its ancestors' choices, as well as engages in behaviours that significantly impact on subsequent peoples. Suzuki thus advocates for the revitalisation of traditional Indigenous worldviews which see ecological sustainability as a way of being a caretaker for the entire system (that is, Earth, the universe, and even the cosmos). Many nature writers also describe the environment as an intricate 'web' in which all life is connected and constantly communicating. Such notions of entirety (or wholeness) and interconnectedness are highly relevant to the concept of Infinity.

Suzuki dedicates *The Sacred Balance* to an exploration of the substances that support all life: air, water, earth, and fire. He says that each element makes the planet habitable, thus humans must acknowledge their intertwined relationship with them. He describes air as an invisible force that surrounds, and gives life to, everything. Of enormous spiritual significance is that the Latin source of the word 'air' is 'spiritus' (meaning the soul, intelligence, essence, or animating principle). As air has no borders or owners, it is shared by all life on Earth: it binds together everything as a single entity extending through time and space. Suzuki notes that water also defies human boundaries. It passes through the air as vapour; it crosses artificially constructed countries and national zones as rivers and oceans; and it trickles through soil, seeping into underground basins. Earth, meanwhile, is the source of fertility and food, and hence all life. The cyclical nature of existence is realised in the process of decaying forms going on to provide nourishment for everything that grows in the soil, as well as those who then consume its produce. Finally, David Suzuki identifies the sun as 'the engine' that drives life on Earth. He describes it as sacred fire, and says that it was light that started the flow of energy that made life possible (growth, movement, and metabolism cannot occur without photons from the sun). Ultimately, without air, water, earth, and sunlight, survival on the planet would simply not happen, so humanity must work to protect and conserve each of them in all their forms.

Suzuki further argues that life is not a passive recipient of these elements, but rather an active participant in creating and replenishing them. For instance, he regards humans as an integral part of the hydrologic cycle - absorbing, storing, and releasing large quantities of water, thereby actively shaping weather and climate. Other nature writers also emphasise the concept of interdependence in light of there being a single living system in which humans must recognise their close relationship with the seasons, animals, and all the elements. Respecting and preserving all parts of nature (such as by maintaining biodiversity) is thus crucial, as humans are part of a greater whole and need to realise that their actions affect everyone and everything. There is no doubt that degrading or destroying any aspect of nature can threaten humanity's own survival. Notions of interdependence, one system, a greater whole, and individual actions affecting everything else are all, then, fundamental to deeper understandings of Infinity.

Connecting to Infinity Through Nature

Another effective way to comprehend Infinity is to regularly visit natural places that have great energetic resonance. There are numerous places on the planet that can provide a true sense of the vastness of Infinity: the mountains of the Himalayas; the glaciers of Antarctica; the big skies of Montana. In an enormous, but largely unoccupied, continent like Australia, an individual can simply sit and contemplate the horizon in landscapes that are mammoth in scale (huge internal deserts and massive all-surrounding oceans). By hiking through rainforests or swimming in reef areas, humans can come to an acute awareness and appreciation of the sheer expansiveness of nature. Through conceptual extension, then, nature itself can provide a metaphorical understanding of the endlessness of Infinity.

The Benefits of Developing a Conception of Infinity
There are a wide range of spiritual, psychological, emotional, and physiological benefits resulting from developing a greater conception of Infinity (that is, a deeper awareness, comprehension, understanding, and appreciation of it as an all-encompassing reality). Emotional balance can replace turmoil if individuals have a more expansive sense of Infinity and do not feel compelled to respond, or over-react, to every life drama. Furthermore, debilitating emotions like grief can be rapidly released through understanding that physical death is not final (the energy of the departed is always accessible on the Earth plane if their guidance is needed). Staying calm, centred, and moving beyond the limits of Earth-bound egos or 'I'-separateness (manifested in the form of insecurities, fears, and guilt complexes) can have the additional benefit of diminishing stress. Consequently, this reduces physical pain (bodily discomfort, illness, and disease), as well as psychological suffering (existential angst, depression, anxiety, and other forms of mental anguish or mental health issues).

*The wide-ranging survey of philosophies in this Appendix should make it clear that the Infinity concept is common to a very large number of languages, cultures, disciplines, and faiths – its universality could, then, imbue it with the power of unity to help create a better world.

APPENDIX C
DIETARY GUIDELINES

The daily recommended dietary intakes for adults are featured below. The lower and upper recommended amounts vary according to gender and age. Please consult the full version of the *Australian Dietary Guidelines: Providing the Scientific Evidence for Healthier Australian Diets* compiled by the National Health and Medical Research Council (published in 2013 under the Australian Government's Department of Health and Ageing). [NB Foods in key groups contain a unique mix of nutrients (vitamins, minerals, and healthy fats), so vegetarian and vegan diets need to ensure adequate *intake* of iron, zinc, calcium, and vitamin B12, as well as adequate *absorption* of them.] *Consume whole foods and minimally processed foods whenever possible.

Plain Water (Consume More When Needed to Stay Hydrated)
- Males: 2.6L (10 cups) per day. Females: 2.1L (8 cups) per day.

Fruit and Vegetables
- 5-6 serves of vegetables and legumes / beans per day (75g per serve, or 100-350kJ). Should include: 1. Half a cup of cooked green, *Brassica*, or cruciferous vegetables. 2. Half a cup of cooked orange vegetables. 3. Half a cup of cooked dried or canned beans, chickpeas, or lentils. 4. 75g of cooked starchy vegetables (potato, sweet potato, taro, sweet corn, or cassava). 5. One cup of raw leafy green vegetables. 6. 75g of other vegetables (e.g., tomato).
- 2 serves of fruit per day (150g total). Can include: 150g (one piece) of medium-sized fruit (for example, apple, banana, orange, pear) *or* 150g (two pieces) of small fruit (for example, apricots, kiwi fruit, plums) *or* 150g (one cup) of diced, cooked, or canned fruit (no added sugar) *or* 125ml (half a cup) of 100% fruit juice (no added sugar) *or* 30g of dried fruit (for example, four dried apricot halves, one and a half tablespoons of sultanas) [the latter two options should only be used as an occasional substitute].

Grain (Cereal) Foods: Mostly Wholegrain and / or High Cereal Fibre Varieties (i.e., Unprocessed and Unrefined Grains / Cereals)
- 4-6 serves per day of breads, cereals, rice, pasta, noodles, polenta, couscous, oats, quinoa, and / or barley (serve size: 500kJ).
- Examples of serves include: 1 slice of bread *or* ½ a medium roll or flat bread (40g); ½ cup of cooked rice, pasta, noodles, barley, buckwheat, semolina, polenta, bulgur, or quinoa

(75–120g); ½ cup of cooked porridge (120g); ¼ cup muesli (30g); 3 crispbreads (35g); and 1 crumpet (60g) *or* 1 small English muffin (35g).

Lean Meats and Alternatives
- 2-3 serves (each 500-600kJ) per day of lean meats, poultry, fish, seafood, eggs, and / or plant-based alternatives (tofu, tempeh, nuts, seeds, beans, and legumes like lentils and chickpeas).
- Examples of serves include: 65g of cooked (90–100g raw weight) lean red meats (e.g., beef, lamb, pork, venison, kangaroo); 80g of cooked (100g raw weight) poultry (e.g., chicken, turkey); 100g (115g raw weight) of cooked fish fillet *or* 1 small can of fish (no added salt); 2 large eggs (120g); 1 cup (150g) of cooked dried beans, lentils, chickpeas, split peas, or canned beans; 170g of tofu; and 30g of nuts or seeds [an occasional substitute only].

Milk, Yoghurt, Cheese and / or Alternatives (Mostly Reduced Fat)
- 2.5-4 serves (each 500-600kJ) per day of milk, yoghurt, cheese, and / or calcium fortified plant-based alternatives.
- Examples of serves include: 1 cup (250ml) of milk (fresh, UHT long life, or reconstituted powdered); 3/4 cup (200g) of yoghurt; 40g (two 4 x 3 x 2 cm pieces) of hard cheese; 1/2 cup (120g) of ricotta cheese; 1 cup (250ml) of soy, rice, oat, or other cereal drink (with at least 100mg of added calcium per 100ml).

Unsaturated Spreads and Oils
- 2-4 serves (each 250kJ) per day of unsaturated spreads and oils.
- Examples of serves include: 10g of polyunsaturated or monosaturated spread; 7g of monounsaturated or polyunsaturated oil (e.g., olive, canola, or sunflower oil); and 10g of tree nuts or peanuts or nut pastes / butter (no added salt).

Limit (or Eliminate)

Alcohol and foods containing saturated fats (baked sweets and junk / fried foods); added salt (savoury processed foods); added sugars (confectionary, soft drinks, fruit drinks, vitamin waters, energy drinks, and sport drinks) should be greatly limited (or even eliminated). Replace foods containing saturated fats (butter, cream, cooking margarine, coconut, and palm oils) with polyunsaturated and monounsaturated fats (oils, nut butters / pastes, and avocado). Salt should be limited to 460-920mg per day (and definitely no more than 1600-2300mg per day). [*Use health-promoting herbs, spices, garlic, lemon juice, and vinegar as forms of seasoning instead of salt.]

APPENDIX D

This publication does not in any way advocate the use of substances that put the physical, mental, or emotional well-being of individuals at risk. A small number of the sources cited in this text feature information about the use of certain substances as a path to accessing 'consciousness' in monitored environments. The vast majority of the referenced sources very strongly claim, however, that no chemically-based mind-altering substances should be used by individuals in any way or at any time. James Van Praagh provides the greatest insight on such matters when he explains that alcohol and drugs should never be used because they provide uncontrollable entries into (and exits out of) altered states, and they attract negative (bad or lower-level) entities. He also emphasises that the development of skills like heightened intuition should be done in a natural and gradual way (by progressively raising one's vibratory rate over a period of time) so that the individual does not suffer from any physical or psychological problems. He is very clear about the fact that a person must at all times be in complete control when opening and closing their energy centres, and this cannot be achieved whilst under the influence of chemical substances.

Extensive medical evidence confirms that there are many problems associated with substance use and abuse. Statistically, substance abuse results in extremely high rates of psychological breakdown and mental illness, as well as massively increased risks of violence, relationship trauma, suicide, financial ruin, addiction, and serious legal problems (including incarceration). Those writers who in any way condone the use of illicit substances (including plant-derived psychedelics) also consistently fail to mention the tragic impacts that high rates of Western drug consumption are having on Indigenous communities, as well as the immense environmental degradation that such actions are wreaking worldwide. Economically disadvantaged peoples and geographical regions (particularly in Asia and Central and South America) are being extensively exploited and destroyed in order to grow and transport drugs, and to otherwise facilitate the supply demands of wealthy Westerners. While substance users focus on their personal interests and agendas, large tracts of jungle are being cleared and countless thousands of individuals are being threatened and killed in the name of the drug trade.

THE PHYSICAL, PSYCHOLOGICAL, AND SOCIAL EFFECTS OF SUBSTANCE USE AND ABUSE

The information in this section has been primarily sourced from the Australian Government site *Health Direct* (www.healthdirect.gov.au); *Medical News Today* (www.medicalnewstoday.com); and *Healthfully* (https://healthfully.com). Each section features only a small sample of the common short-term, bad reaction, and long-term detrimental effects associated with consumption of the identified substances. Additional research is recommended.

Cannabis (Marijuana and Hashish): Increased heart rate; nausea; decreased reaction times; poor balance; lack of coordination; red eyes; dry mouth and throat; vomiting; anxiety; mood swings; serious memory loss; dependency; paranoia; depression; loss of sex drive; learning difficulties; suicidal thoughts; chest infections (asthma and bronchitis); irregular periods in women; lower sperm count in men; psychosis; schizophrenia.

Plant-Derived Psychedelics (Ayahuasca, Ibogaine, Huachuma, Psilocybin Mushrooms, and so on): Nausea; vomiting; loss of appetite; diarrhoea; profuse sweating; tremors; increased heart rate and blood pressure; elevated body temperature; muscular spasms, weakness, and incoordination; rapid breathing; dry mouth; dilated pupils; dizziness; drowsiness; impaired concentration; disorientation; disengagement; altered perception; distorted thinking; agitation; memory problems; disturbed sleep; inability to move; seizures; fear; paranoia; confusion; anxiety; panic; delirium; depression; psychosis; schizophrenia; long-term blurred eyesight; frightening and prolonged visual and auditory hallucinations; suicidality; death.

LSD (Acid): Nausea; vomiting; headaches; increased heart rate and blood pressure; muscle twitching; dizziness; confusion; insomnia; sweating or chills; abdominal pain; seizures; extreme anxiety, fear, or panic; dangerous acts of risk-taking; paranoia; loss of control; frightening hallucinations; permanent insanity.

Alcohol: Vomiting; headaches; dizziness; confusion; mood swings; poor concentration; feelings of despair; anger; aggression; impaired judgement; loss of memory; lack of coordination; fatigue; alcohol poisoning; foetal damage in pregnant women; accidental injury or deliberate harm (to self and / or others); dependence; addiction;

anxiety; depression; increased risk of suicide; weight gain; reduction of testosterone levels, sperm count, and fertility for men; erratic menstruation for women; increased risk of strokes, dementia, blood pressure, heart damage, heart attacks, liver cirrhosis, liver cancer, stomach ulcers, stomach cancer, and bowel cancer.

MDMA (Ecstasy): Dilated pupils; increased blood pressure and heartbeat; very high temperature; vomiting; jaw clenching; teeth grinding; sweating; nausea; muscle aches and pains; confusion; irritability; anxiety; exhaustion; aggression; paranoia; convulsions; irrational behaviour; extreme agitation; cracked teeth; nerve damage; exacerbation of serious mental illnesses.

Cocaine: Dilated pupils; increased temperature; high blood pressure; poor concentration; headaches; dizziness; restlessness; chest pains; extreme mood swings; exhaustion; irritability; paranoia; severe anxiety; agitation; seizures and strokes (leading to cardiac arrest and death); diminished mental function; long-term loss of motivation and interest in sex (as well as impaired sexual performance); bronchitis; fits; damage to the septum of the nose; hallucinations; psychosis; financial problems; risk of strokes, heart disease, and kidney failure.

Amphetamines (Speed): Nausea; vomiting; enlarged pupils; loss of memory and concentration; increased blood pressure, heart rate, and breathing (difficulties); nervousness; dry mouth; chills or fever; jaw clenching; teeth grinding; confusion; mood swings; paranoia; seizures; convulsions; passing out; no urine output; depression; irritability; severe anxiety; panic attacks; hallucinations; sleeping problems; violent behaviour; serious mental health illnesses.

Heroin (and Other Opioids): Slowed breathing; poor concentration; low body temperature; slow heartbeat; itchiness; difficulty urinating; slurred speech; muscle twitching; blue lips and nails; seizures, stroke, and cardiac arrest (leading to coma and death); mood swings; anxiety; depression; multiple physical and mental health illnesses; addiction; suicidality; serious financial and legal problems (incarceration).

Methamphetamines (Ice, Crystal Meth, and so on): Heart palpitations; breathing problems; confusion; severe headaches; poor concentration; seizures; uncontrolled jerking; agitation; extreme weight loss; dental issues; nosebleeds; stiff muscles; insomnia; frequent colds; kidney and heart problems; depression; stroke; addiction; suicidality; death.

APPENDIX E
STRATEGIES FOR CLEARING NEGATIVE ENERGIES

In *Minding Your Mind: Understanding Your Mind, Taking Control of Your Mental Health* (2022, Penguin Australia), Ian Hickie and James O'Loghlin have compiled a list of the top strategies that individuals can employ to ensure personal happiness. These include having a passion; being involved in a higher cause; ending egocentric forms of narcissism; identifying the causes of daily happiness; acting happy (such as by telling positive stories); developing harmonious intimate relationships; and living in the moment (by detaching from the past, being open to change, and focusing on new opportunities).

The following strategies can also be utilised to shift old energies and to subsequently invite (or seek out) new, healthier energies. These approaches can involve the clearing of damaging physical addictions, unproductive mental patterns, and negative emotions. The ideas listed below may provide quick stimulus for shifting and clearing negative energies, or they may be a platform to engaging in deeper personal transformation.

1. Step Into Your Fears With Consciousness
2. Put Your Difficult Experiences Into a Wider Context
3. Connect With Those Who Make You Feel Valued and Loved
4. Know Your Vulnerabilities and Ways to Stay Protected
5. Transform Your Emotions Into Artistic Expression
6. Maintain Your Faith in People
7. Read and View Historical Accounts of Survival
8. Determine Why Your Subconscious Mind Attracted Difficulties
9. Know That Your Situation Is Not the End of the World
10. Eliminate All Unnecessary Stresses and Dramas
11. Determine Where You Are Wasting Time and Energy in Life
12. Compose a Poem About a Symbolic Movement From Grief to Joy
13. Identify Your Self-Sabotaging Thinking and Behavioural Patterns
14. Seek Closure
15. Process Revenge Fantasies in a Psychologically Healthy Way
16. Brainstorm Solutions to Your Problems
17. Analyse Strengths and Weaknesses in Your Former Relationships

18. Write Old Relationships Out of Your System
19. Confront Lingering Issues With People From Your Past
20. Consider What a Healed Version of You Will Be Like
21. Read Widely on Matters of Psychology and Self-Help
22. Look to Your Body to Provide Answers to Your Problems
23. Consciously Turn All Negative Thoughts Into Positive Statements
24. Seek Healing Through Dream Analysis
25. Use Multiple Perspectives to Define Your Experiences
26. Seek Out Relaxation or Healing Centres and Workshops
27. Focus on Holistic Healing of Your Body, Mind, and Soul
28. Find a Sense of Purity and Joy in Simple Forms of Fun
29. Seek Guidance From People You Trust
30. Take Up a New Hobby or Social Activity
31. Travel or See the Local Sights
32. Seek Out Intellectual Stimulation
33. Enjoy a Make-Over and Cultivate New Friendships
34. Foster Hope for Healthier Future Relationships
35. Ask the Universe to Send You a Teacher or Guide
36. Take Risks and Do Things You've Never Done Before
37. Move to a New Location
38. Seek Out Natural and Alternative Forms of Healing
39. Plan Out Your Day to Bring You Maximum Happiness
40. Identify What You Will Not Tolerate in Future Relationships
41. Learn About the Nature of Energy and Other New Age Concepts
42. Take Guidance From Indigenous Cultures and Elders
43. Engage in Creative Visualisation Activities
44. Make Peace With Your Life Experiences
45. Engage in Confidence-Building and Empowerment Activities
46. Turn to the Masters for a Deeper Understanding of Life
47. Smile, Give Thanks, Be Happy, and Live the Good Life
48. Embark on an Inner Journey into Self-Awareness
49. Take Greater Note of Synchronicities and Signs
50. Develop Your Intuition
51. Embark on a Spiritual Journey
52. Do What You Love and Take Steps to Pursue Your Soul Purpose
53. Use Your Personal Experiences to Counsel Others
54. Be Your Best Self
55. Turn Negative Life Experiences Into Positive Opportunities

BIBLIOGRAPHY

Adcock, Will (2000) *Shamanism: Rituals for Spiritual Journeying and Creating Sacred Space.* London: Anness.

Albert, David (1992) *Quantum Mechanics and Experience.* Cambridge: Harvard University Press.

The Alchemist (2020) 'Five Secrets of the Infinity Symbol'. *Mind Journal:* https://themindsjournal.com.

Alexander, Eben (2012) *Proof of Heaven: A Neurosurgeon's Journey Into the Afterlife.* Sydney: Macmillan Australia.

Alexander, Eben (2014) *The Map of Heaven: How Science, Religion, and Ordinary People Are Proving the Afterlife.* New York: Simon & Schuster.

Allen, Marc (1998) *A Visionary Life: Conversations on Creating the Life You Want.* Novato (CA): New World Library.

Anderson, Jane (1998) *The Shape of Things to Come: Predicting the Future.* Sydney: Random House.

Angelical Balance (2022) '9 Infinity Symbol Spiritual Meanings'. www.angelicalbalance.com.

Arienta, Sahvanna (2019) *Lightworker's Guide to the Astral Realm.* Newburyport (MA): Weiser Books.

Arntz, William et al (Dir.) (2006) *What the Bleep Do We Know!?: Down the Rabbit Hole.* United States of America: Captured Light.

The AstroTwins (2022) 'North and South Nodes: The Astrology of Your Life Purpose and Past Lives'. *Astrostyle:* https://astrostyle.com.

Baggott, Andy (1999) *Runes: For Divination, Protection, and Healing.* London: Anness.

Baggott, Andy (1999) *Celtic Wisdom.* London: Piatkus.

Balogh, Penelope (1971) *Freud: A Biographical Introduction.* New York: Charles Scribner's Sons.

Banaszak, Doreen (2007) *Excuse Me, Your Life is Now: Mastering the Law of Attraction.* Charlottesville (VA): Hampton.

Banzhaf, Hajo and Theler, Brigitte (1998) *Secrets of Love and Partnership: The Astrological Guide for Finding Your 'One and Only'.* York Beach (ME): Samuel Weiser.

Bartlett, Sarah (2006) *The Tarot Bible: The Definitive Guide to the Cards and Spreads.* London: Godsfield Press.

Beare, Hedley and Slaughter, Richard (1993) *Education for the Twenty-First Century.* London: Routledge.

Beresford, Quentin et al (Eds) (2003) *Reform and Resistance in Aboriginal Education: The Australian Experience.* Perth: University of Western Australia Press.

Bethards, Betty (1995) *The Dream Book: Symbols for Self-Understanding.* Rockport (MA): Element.

Blackwell Lawrence, Shirley (2019) *The Big Book of Numerology: The Hidden Meaning of Numbers and Letters.* Newburyport (MA): Weiser Books.

Bodine, Michael (2018) *A Psychic's Life: What It's Really Like.* Minnesota: Llewellyn Worldwide.

Boice, Judith (1989) *At One With All Life: A Personal Journey in Gaian Communities.* Forres (Scotland): Findhorn Press.

Boulding, Elise (1990) *Building a Global Civic Culture: Education for an Interdependent World.* Syracuse: University Press.

Bourke, Colin et al (Eds) (1994) *Aboriginal Australia.* Brisbane: University of Queensland Press.

Boyer, William H. (2002) *Education for the Twenty-First Century.* San Francisco: Caddo Gap Press.

Boyle, Mark (2019) *The Way Home: Tales From a Life Without Technology.* London: Oneworld Publications.

Brandt, Ronald S. (Ed.) (2000) *Education in a New Era.* Alexandria (VA): ASCD.

Brinkley, Dannion and Brinkley, Kathryn (2008) *Secrets of the Light: Lessons from Heaven.* London: Piatkus.

Brown, Matthew (Dir.) (2016) *The Man Who Knew Infinity.* The United Kingdom: Pressman Film et al.

Buenfil, Alberto Ruiz (1991) *Rainbow Nation Without Borders: Toward an Ecotopian Millennium.* Santa Fe (NM): Bear.

Burbules, Nicholas and Torres, Carlos (2000) *Globalisation and Education: Critical Perspectives.* New York: Routledge.

Burger, Julian (1990) *The Gaian Atlas of First Peoples: A Future for the Indigenous World.* New York: Anchor Books.

Byrne, Rhonda (2006) *The Secret.* New York: Atria Books.

Callaghan, Paul and Gordon, Uncle Paul (2022) *The Dreaming Path: Indigenous Thinking to Change Your Life.* Sydney: Pantera Press.

Campbell, Rebecca (2015) *Light is the New Black: A Guide to Answering Your Soul's Callings.* Carlsbad (CA): Hay House.

Capra, Fritjof (1975) *The Tao of Physics: An Exploration of the Parallels Between Modern Physics and Eastern Mysticism.* Boulder (CO): Shambhala Publications.

Carlson, Richard (1997) *Don't Sweat the Small Stuff: Simple Ways to Keep the Little Things From Taking Over Your Life.* Sydney: Bantam.
Cherry, Kendra (2020) 'What is a Digital Detox?' *Very Well Mind:* https://www.verywellmind.com.
Cheung, Theresa (2008) *Working With Your Sixth Sense: Practical Ways to Develop Your Intuition.* London: Godsfield Press.
Chopra, Deepak (1993) *Ageless Body, Timeless Mind: A Practical Alternative to Growing Old.* Sydney: Random House.
Chopra, Deepak (2005) *SynchroDestiny: Harnessing the Infinite Power of Coincidences to Create Miracles.* London: Rider-Trade.
Chopra, Deepak (2006) *Life After Death: The Book of Answers.* London: Rider.
Chopra, Deepak (2009) *The Ultimate Happiness Prescription: 7 Keys to Joy and Enlightenment.* London: Rider.
Choquette, Sonia (2007) *Soul Lessons and Soul Purpose: A Channelled Guide to Why You Are Here.* Carlsbad (CA): Hay House.
Christoff, Peter (Ed.) (2014) *Four Degrees of Global Warming: Australia in a Hot World.* New York: Routledge.
Collard, L. et al (2013) *Mooro Nyoongar Katitjin Bidi (Mooro People's Knowledge Trail).* Perth: City of Stirling.
Conneeley, Serene and Stanley, Tamara (Compilers) (2007) *20 Hay House Classics.* Sydney: Hay House Australia.
Control Your Mindset (2022) 'What is the Meaning of Infinity and Beyond?' https://controlyourmindset.com.
Cook, Trevor (1995) *Black on White: Policy and Curriculum Development in Aboriginal Education.* Sydney: Human Factors Press.
Coombes, Mitchell (2019) *Signs From Spirit: Inspiring True Stories From the Afterlife.* Sydney: Brio Books.
Coombs, Herbert Cole (1994) *Aboriginal Autonomy: Issues and Strategies.* Cambridge: Cambridge University Press.
Cooper, Diana (2007) *A Little Light on the Spiritual Laws.* Forres (Scotland): Findhorn Press.
Craven, Rhonda (Ed.) (2000). *Aboriginal Studies: Self-concept for a Nation.* ASA Conference: University of Western Sydney.
Cremo, Michael et al (1997) *Chant and Be Happy: The Power of Mantra Meditation.* Los Angeles: Bhaktivedanta Book Trust.
Cunningham, Bailey (2002) *Mandala: Journey to the Centre.* London: Dorling Kindersley.

The Dalai Lama (1989) *Ocean of Wisdom: Guideline for Living.* Santa Fe (NM): Clear Light.

Day, Laura (2006) *Welcome to Your Crisis: How to Use the Power of Crisis to Create the Life You Want.* New York: Little Brown.

Day, Laura (2010) *How to Rule the World From Your Couch: The Power of Intuition.* New York: Atria Books.

Delbridge, Arthur (Ed.) (1990) *The Macquarie Encyclopaedic Dictionary.* Sydney: Macquarie Library.

Dictionary by Merriam-Webster (2022) 'Definition of Infinity'. Encyclopaedia Britannica: www.merriam-webster.com.

Dictionary.com (2018) 'What Does Infinity Symbol Mean?' www.dictionary.com.

Dispenza, Joe (2012) *Breaking the Habit of Being Yourself: How to Lose Your Mind and Create a New One.* Carlsbad (CA): Hay House.

Dispenza, Joe (2017) *Becoming Supernatural: How Common People Are Doing the Uncommon.* Carlsbad (CA): Hay House.

Dow, Kirstin and Downing, Thomas (2006) *The Atlas of Climate Change.* London: Earthscan.

Dowling, Ken (2012) *Universal Symbols: Keys to Your Consciousness.* Sunshine Coast (Qld): Balboa Press.

Dyer, Wayne (1978) *Pulling Your Own Strings: Dynamic Techniques for Dealing With Other People and Living Your Life As You Choose.* New York: Harper Collins.

Dyer, Wayne (1992) *Real Magic: Creating Miracles in Everyday Life.* Sydney: Harper Collins.

Dyer, Wayne (2005) *You'll See It When You Believe It: The Way to Your Personal Transformation.* London: Random House.

Dyer, Wayne (2006) *Being in Balance: 9 Principles for Creating Habits to Match Your Desires.* Carlsbad (CA): Hay House.

Dyer, Wayne (2009) *Stop the Excuses!: How to Change Lifelong Thoughts.* Carlsbad (CA): Hay House.

Dyer, Wayne (2010) *The Shift: Taking Your Life from Ambition to Meaning.* Carlsbad (CA): Hay House.

Eason, Cassandra (2005) *Contact Your Spirit Guides to Enrich Your Life.* London: Quantum.

Eckersley, Richard (2004) *Well and Good: How We Feel and Why It Matters.* Melbourne: Text Publishing.

The Editors of Encyclopaedia Britannica (2022) 'Zeno of Elea'. *Encyclopaedia Britannica:* www.britannica.com.

Edward, John (2010) *Infinite Quest: Develop Your Psychic Intuition to Take Charge of Your Life.* New York: Sterling.
Egger, Gary and Swinburn, Boyd (2010) *Planet Obesity: How We're Eating Ourselves and The Planet to Death.* Sydney: Allen & Unwin.
Emoto, Masaru (2005) *The Hidden Messages in Water.* New York: Atria Books.
Enright, Gabbie (2008) *Living the Light: Discovering Truth and Living in Spirit.* Adelaide: Peacock Publications.
Erwin, Kerrie (2019) *Clearing: Your Guide to Maintaining Energy.* Sydney: Rockpool Publishing.
Famous Scientists: The Art of Genius (2018) 'John Wallis'. www.famousscientists.org.
Farrell, Mary (2005) *Acts of Trust: Making Sense of Risk, Trust, and Betrayal in Our Relationships.* Wollombi (NSW): Exisle.
Faruzo (2022) 'Infinity Symbol – Infinity Symbolism Meaning and History'. www.faruzo.com.
Feuerstein, Georg and Feuerstein, Brenda (2007) *Green Yoga.* Saskatchewan: Traditional Yoga Studies.
Fields, Zoe-Anne (2015) *Transformations: A Guided Journal.* Fremantle: Vivid Publishing.
Flannery, Tim (2003) *Beautiful Lies: Population and Environment in Australia.* Melbourne: Griffin Press.
Folds, Ralph (1987) *Whitefella School: Education and Aboriginal Resistance.* Sydney: Allen & Unwin.
Ford, Debbie (2008) *Why Good People Do Bad Things: How to Stop Being Your Own Worst Enemy.* New York: Harper Collins.
Frankl, Viktor (2006) *Man's Search for Meaning: An Introduction to Logotherapy.* Boston: Beacon.
Freire, Paulo (1972) *Cultural Action for Freedom.* Cambridge (MA): Penguin.
Frekey, Timothy (Ed.) (1998) *The Wisdom of the Hindu Gurus.* North Clarendon (VT): Tuttle Publishing.
Garth, Maureen (1994) *The Inner Garden: Meditations for Life From 9 to 90.* Melbourne: Collins Dove.
Gawain, Shakti (1986) *Living in the Light: A Guide to Personal and Planetary Transformation.* San Rafael (CA): Whatever Publishing.
Gawain, Shakti (1989) *Return to the Garden: A Journey of Discovery.* San Rafael (CA): New World Library.

Gawain, Shakti (2000) *The Path of Transformation: How Healing Ourselves Can Change the World.* Novato (CA): Nataraj.

Gawain, Shakti (2002) *Developing Intuition: Practical Guidance for Daily Life.* Novato (CA): New World Books.

Gawler, Ian (1987) *Peace of Mind: How You Can Learn to Meditate and Use the Power of Your Mind.* Melbourne: Hill of Content.

Gendlin, Eugene (1978) *Focusing.* London: Everest House.

Gilbert, Elizabeth (2006) *Eat, Pray, Love: One Woman's Search for Everything.* London: Bloomsbury Paperbacks.

Gilbert, Elizabeth (2010) *Committed: A Skeptic Makes Peace With Marriage.* New York: Viking Press.

Gilbert, Elizabeth (2015) *Big Magic: Creative Living Beyond Fear.* London: Bloomsbury Paperbacks.

Ginny (2018) 'Infinity Symbol Meaning – What Does Infinity Mean?'. https://blog.centimegift.com.

Goldberg, Philip (1983) *The Intuitive Edge: Understanding Intuition and Applying it in Life.* Los Angeles: Tarcher.

Gordon, Anita and Suzuki, David (1990) *It's A Matter of Survival.* Toronto: Stoddart.

Grace, Liliane (2006) *The Mastery Club: See the Invisible, Hear the Silent, Do the Impossible.* Mt Waverley (VIC): Grace Productions.

Green, Reinaldo Marcus (Dir.) (2021) *King Richard.* United States of America: Westbrook Studios et al.

Greer, Germaine (2003) *Whitefella Jump Up: The Shortest Way to Nationhood* (Quarterly Essay). Melbourne: Schwartz Publishing.

Gribbin, John (2020) 'The Many-Worlds Theory, Explained'. *The MIT Press Reader:* https://thereader.mitpress.mit.edu.

Groome, Howard (1995) *Working Purposefully with Aboriginal Students.* Sydney: Social Science Press.

Guggenheimer, Amanda (2011) *The Light-Worker's Companion: A Gateway into Higher Realms and the Dimensions of Consciousness.* Australia: Arcadia Press.

Gyllen (2019) 'Infinity Symbol Meaning in Modern Times'. Stockholm: https://gyllenwatches.com.

Hajkiowicz, Stefan (2015) *Global Megatrends: Seven Patterns of Change Shaping our Future.* Melbourne: CSIRO Publishing.

Hargreaves, Andy et al (1996) *Schooling for Change: Reinventing Education for Early Adolescents.* London: Falmer Press.

Harris, Philip (1993) *The Spiritual Path to Complete Fulfilment.* Melbourne: Hill of Content.

Harris, Stephen (1990) *Two Ways Aboriginal Schooling: Education and Cultural Survival*. Canberra: Aboriginal Studies Press.
Harrison, Eric (1993) *Teach Yourself to Meditate: Over 20 Simple Exercises for Peace, Health, and Clarity of Mind.* Sydney: Simon & Schuster.
Harrison, Stephanie and Kleiner, Barbara (1999) *Crystal Wisdom for Personal Growth: Discover How to Fulfil Your Mental, Emotional, and Spiritual Potential*. Sydney: Simon & Schuster.
Hartley, Anne (2000) *Love the Life You Live: Ten Steps for Happier Living.* Mona Vale: Hart Publishing.
Hartmann, Thom (2001) *The Prophet's Way: Touching the Power of Life.* Sydney: Bantam.
Hawes, Martin (2003) *Twelve Principles for Living with Integrity in the Twenty-First Century.* Sydney: Finch Publishing.
Hawker, Paul (1998) *Soul Survivor: A Spiritual Quest Through 40 Days and 40 Nights of Mountain Solitude.* Kelowna (BC): Northstone Publishing.
Hawking, Stephen W. (1988) *A Brief History of Time: From The Big Bang to Black Holes.* London: Random House.
Hay, Louise (1987) *You Can Heal Your Life.* Concord (NSW): Specialist Publications.
Haydon, Graham (1997) *Teaching About Values: A New Approach.* London: Cassell.
Hewitt, Alan (2007) *A Perfect Calm.* Perth: Earth Star.
Hillman, James (1996) *The Soul's Code: In Search of Character and Calling.* New York: Random House.
Hof, Wim (2020) *The Wim Hof Method: Activate Your Potential, Transcend Your Limits.* London: Random House.
Holzner, Steven (2013) *Quantum Physics for Dummies.* Hoboken (NJ): Wiley.
Howell, Cate (2013) *Intuition: Unlock the Power!* Wollombi (NSW): Exisle Publishing.
Hutchinson, Francis (1996) *Educating Beyond Violent Futures.* London: Routledge.
Hyde, Maggie and McGuinness, Michael (1999) *Introducing Jung.* London: Icon Books.
IDL (In Different Languages) (2013-2022) 'How to Say Infinity In Different Languages'. Igor Katsev: www.indifferentlanguages.com.
Illich, Ivan (1973) *Deschooling Society.* London: Penguin.

Ingold, Tim et al (Eds) (1988) *Hunters and Gatherers: Property, Power and Ideology*. New York: Berg.
Integral+Life (2008) *Integral Spirituality* (DVD). Boulder (CO): Integral Life.
Jackson, Anthony and Davis, Gayle (2000) *Turning Points 2000: Educating Adolescents in the 21st Century*. New York: Teachers College Press.
James, Marc and Klein, Dhyan (1988) *The Practical Guide to Crystal Healing*. Melbourne: Gemcraft.
Johnson, Robert A. (1983) *The Psychology of Romantic Love*. London: Arkana.
Jung, Carl Gustav (1961) *Man and His Symbols*. London: Random House.
Jung, Carl Gustav (1961) *Memories, Dreams, Reflections*. London: Random House.
Kanigel, Robert (1991) *The Man Who Knew Infinity: A Life of the Genius Ramanujan*. New York: Charles Scribner's Sons.
Keen, Ian (2004) *Aboriginal Economy and Society: Australia at the Threshold of Colonisation*. Oxford: Oxford University Press.
King, Petrea (2004) *Your Life Matters: The Power of Living Now*. Sydney: Random House.
Kingma, Daphne Rose (1998) *The Future of Love: The Power of the Soul in Intimate Relationships*. New York: Broadway Books.
Kingma, Daphne Rose (2010) *The Ten Things to Do When Your Life Falls Apart: An Emotional and Spiritual Handbook*. Novato (CA): New World Library.
Knudtson, Peter and Suzuki, David (1992) *Wisdom of the Elders: Sacred Native Stories of Nature*. Toronto: Stoddart.
Kohen, James (1995). *Aboriginal Environmental Impacts*. Sydney: University of New South Wales Press.
Krull, Wilhelm (Ed.) (2000) *Debates on Issues of our Common Future*. Germany: Velbruck Wissenschaft.
Kwan, Dan and Scheinert, Daniel (Directors) (2022) *Everything Everywhere All At Once*. United States of America: AGBO et al.
Laszlo, Ervin (2021) *The Immutable Laws of The Akashic Field: Universal Truths for a Better Life and World*. New York: St Martin's.
Lemin, Marion et al (Eds) (1994) *Values Strategies for Classroom Teachers*. Melbourne: Acer.

Lisman, C. David (1996) *The Curricular Integration of Ethics: Theory and Practice*. London: Praeger.

Lovelock, James (1979) *Gaia: A New Look at Life on Earth*. Oxford: Oxford University Press.

Lucas, George (Dir.) (1977) *Star Wars / Episode IV: A New Hope*. United States of America: Lucasfilm.

Luna, Aletheia and Sol, Mateo (2012-2022) *LonerWolf*. Perth (WA): https://lonerwolf.com.

Luther King, Jr., Martin (1963) *Strength to Love*. Philadelphia: Fortress Press.

McArthur, Bruce (1993) *Your Life: Why It Is the Way It Is and What You Can Do About It – Understanding the Universal Laws*. Virginia Beach: Bruce McArthur.

McBay, Aric et al (2011) *Deep Green Resistance: Strategy to Save the Planet*. New York: Seven Stories Press.

McCartney, John (1992) *Black Power Ideologies*. Philadelphia: Temple University Press.

McConchie, Peter (Ed.) (2003) *Elders: Wisdom from Australia's Indigenous Leaders*. Cambridge: Cambridge University Press.

McDaid, Bernadette et al (Prod.) (2010-2017) *Through the Wormhole*. United States of America: Revelations Entertainment et al.

McGregor, Trish and McGregor, Rob (2011) *The Seven Secrets of Synchronicity: Your Guide to Finding Meaning in Signs Big and Small*. Avon (MA): Adams Media.

McNeill, John (2000) *Something New Under the Sun: An Environmental History of the Twentieth Century*. London: Penguin.

Mandela, Nelson (2010) *Conversations With Myself*. London: Macmillan.

Manos Jr, James (Creator for Television) (2006-2013) *Dexter* (Seasons 1-8). Miami (FL) and Long Beach (CA): The Colleton Company et al.

Margolis, Char (1999) *Questions From Earth, Answers From Heaven: A Psychic Intuitive's Discussion of Life, Death, and What Awaits Us Beyond*. Sydney: Allen & Unwin.

Margolis, Char (2008) *Discover Your Inner Wisdom: Using Intuition, Logic, and Common Sense to Make Your Best Choices*. New York: Allen & Unwin.

Martin, Angela (2002) *Practical Intuition: Practical Tools for Harnessing the Power of Your Instinct*. Sydney: Lansdowne.

Martin, Patricia (Ed.) (1995) *Ancient Echoes: Native American Words of Wisdom*. US: Great Quotations Publishing.

Masters, Geoff (2016) *Five Challenges in Australian School Education*. www.research.acer.edu.au.

Maxwell, John C. (2006) *The Difference Maker: Making Your Attitude Your Greatest Asset*. Nashville (TN): Thomas Nelson.

Mayes, Sherron (2004) *How to Be a Supernatural Lover: Tuning in Your Psychic Powers for Your Best Ever Relationship*. London: Hodder & Stoughton.

Millman, Dan et al (2009) *Bridge Between Worlds: Extraordinary Experiences That Changed Lives*. California: H. J. Kramer.

Milojevic, Ivana (2003) 'When Will We Ever Learn?' *Social Alternatives*, 22 (4), 17-21.

Milojevic, Ivana (2005) *Educational Futures: Dominant and Contesting Visions*. London: Routledge.

Minchin, Nel and Blair, Wayne (Dir.) *Firestarter: The Story of Bangarra*. Sydney: Ivan O'Mahoney (Prod.).

Moore, Thomas (1994) *Soul Mates: Honouring the Mysteries of Love and Relationship*. New York: Harper Collins.

Mueller Shutan, Mary (2015) *The Spiritual Awakening Guide: Kundalini, Psychic Abilities, and The Conditioned Layers of Reality*. Forres (Scotland): Findhorn Press.

Murphy, Joseph (1997) *The Power of Your Subconscious Mind*. London: Pocket Books.

Neu, Jerome (Ed.) (1991) *The Cambridge Companion to Freud*. Cambridge: Cambridge University Press.

Noddings, Nell (1992) *The Challenge to Care in Schools: An Alternative Approach to Education*. New York: Teachers College Press.

Noe, Karen (2014) *Your Life After Their Death: A Medium's Guide to Healing After a Loss*. Carlsbad (CA): Hay House.

Norwood, Robin (1995) *Why Me, Why This, Why Now?: A Guide to Answering Life's Toughest Questions*. London: Arrow Books.

O'Donohue, John (1997) *Anam Cara: Spiritual Wisdom From the Celtic World*. London: Bantam.

O'Donohue, John (1998) *Eternal Echoes: Exploring Our Hunger to Belong*. London: Bantam.

O'Donohue, John (2003) *Divine Beauty: The Invisible Embrace*. London: Bantam.

Orbach, Susie (1994) *What's Really Going On Here?: Making Sense of Our Emotional Lives.* London: Virago Press.
Orr, David (1993) 'Schools for the Twenty-First Century'. *Resurgence,* 160, 16-19.
Parish, D. (1991) 'Aboriginal Worldview in the Educational Context'. *The Aboriginal Child at School*, 19 (4), 14-21.
Partington, Gary (1996) *Hasluck versus Coombs: White Politics and Australia's Aborigines.* Sydney: Quakers Hill Press.
Peat, F. David (1989) *Synchronicity: The Bridge Between Matter and Mind.* New York: Bantam Books.
Peck, M. Scott (1978) *The Road Less Travelled.* London: Arrow Books.
Peirce, Penney (1997) *The Intuitive Way: The Definitive Guide to Increasing Your Awareness.* New York: Atria.
Peru, Elizabeth (2018) *Cosmic Messengers: The Universal Secrets to Unlocking Your Purpose and Becoming Your Own Life Guide.* Sydney: Hay House.
Powers, John. (2007) *Odditude: Finding the Passion for Who You Are and What You Do.* Florida: Health Communications.
Purpel, David (1989) *The Moral and Spiritual Crisis in Education: A Curriculum for Justice and Compassion in Education.* New York: Bergin & Garvey.
Puskas, Grace Gabriella (2021) 'Infinity Symbol Spiritual Meaning: What is its Significance and Symbolism?' https://digestfromexperts.com.
Radin, Dean (1997) *The Conscious Universe: The Scientific Truth of Psychic Phenomena.* San Francisco: HarperOne.
Raff, Jeffrey (2006) *The Practice of Ally Work: Meeting and Partnering With Your Spirit Guide in the Imaginal World.* Lake Worth (FL): Nicolas-Hays.
Raypole, Crystal (2020) 'Ever Been Told You Have an Old Soul? Here's What That Really Means'. *Healthline:* www.healthline.com.
Redfield, James (1993) *The Celestine Prophecy: An Adventure.* Sydney: Bantam Books.
Redfield, James and Adrienne, Carol (1995) *The Celestine Prophecy: An Experiential Guide.* Sydney: Bantam.
Redfield, James (1997) *The Celestine Vision: Living the New Spiritual Awareness.* New York: Grand Central Publishing.
Redfield, James (1999) *The Secret of Shambhala: In Search of the Eleventh Insight.* New York: Warner Books.

Reynolds, Henry (1981) *The Other Side of the Frontier: Aboriginal Resistance to the European Invasion of Australia.* Melbourne: Penguin.

Rhys, Dani (2021) 'Infinity Symbol – Origins, Significance, and Meaning'. *Symbol Sage*: https://symbolsage.com.

Richardson, Tanya Carroll (2009-2022) 'Soul Connection: 12 Types of Soul Mates & How to Recognise Them'. *MindBodyGreen*: https://www.mindbodygreen.com.

Robinson, Lynn et al (2004) *The Complete Idiot's Guide to Psychic Awareness.* Indianapolis: Alpha Books.

Roiss, Sabine (2020) 'Spiritual Meaning of the Infinity Symbol'. *Medium*: https://medium.com.

Roman, Sanaya (2019) *Personal Power Through Awareness: A Guidebook for Sensitive People.* Novato (CA): New World Library.

Ross, Gillian (1993) *The Search for the Pearl: A Personal Exploration of Science and Mysticism.* Sydney: ABC Books.

Rowland, Michael (1993) *Absolute Happiness: The Manual to a Life of Complete Fulfilment and Awakening Your True Power.* Sydney: Self Communications.

Russell, David O. (Dir.) (2004) *I Heart Huckabees.* United States of America: Qwerty Films et al.

Russo-Young, Ry (Dir.) (2017) *Before I Fall.* United States of America: Awesomeness Films et al.

Schuldt, Lori (2007) *Martin Luther King, Jr with profiles of Mohandas K. Gandhi and Nelson Mandela.* Chicago: World Book.

Schwarz, Joyce (2008) *The Vision Board.* New York: Collins Design.

Sinclair, Gerald (2020) 'The True Meaning of the Infinity Symbol'. *Awareness Act:* https://awarenessact.com.

Skinner, Stephen (2000) *Feng Shui.* Bath: Paragon.

Slaughter, Richard (1994) *From Fatalism to Foresight: Educating for the Early 21st Century.* Melbourne: Australian Council for Educational Administration.

Slaughter, Richard (1995) *Futures: Tools and Techniques*. Melbourne: Futures Studies Centre.

Slaughter, Richard (Ed.) (1996) *New Thinking for a New Millennium: The Knowledge Base of Futures Studies*. London: Routledge.

Smith, Gordon (2012) *Intuitive Studies: A Complete Course in Mediumship.* London: Hay House.

Smith, Gordon (2017) *Mediumship: An Introductory Guide to Developing Spiritual Awareness and Intuition.* Carlsbad (CA): Hay House.

Smith, Terry (Ed.) (1999) *First Peoples: Second Chance.* Canberra: The Australian Academy of the Humanities.

Soskin, Julie (2002) *Are you Psychic?* London: Carroll & Brown.

The Spierig Brothers (Directors) (2014) *Predestination.* Australia: Screen Australia et al.

Spiritualify (2019) 'The Spiritual Meaning of the Infinity Symbol! What Are its Powers?' https://blog.spiritualify.com.

Stanner, W. E. H. (1976) 'Aborigines and Australian Society'. *Mankind,* Vol 10, No. 4, pp. 201-212.

Stevenson, Jay (2000) *The Complete Idiot's Guide to Eastern Philosophy: Valuable Tips for Putting Philosophical Theory Into Practice.* Indianapolis (IN): Alpha.

Stuart, Gordon (2000) *The Paranormal: An Illustrated Encyclopaedia.* London: Caxton Publishing Group.

Sullivan, Hugh (Dir.) (2014) *The Infinite Man.* Australia: Hedone Productions et al.

Suni, Eric (2022) 'Healthy Sleep Tips'. *OneCare Media*: www.sleepfoundation.org.

Suzuki, David (1997) *The Sacred Balance: Rediscovering Our Place in Nature.* Vancouver: Greystone Books.

Suzuki, David and Dressel, Holly (2002) *Good News for a Change: How Everyday People Are Helping the Planet.* Toronto: Stoddart.

Sylwester, Eva (2022) 'Infinity Symbol Meaning and Symbolism'. *The Symbolism*: www.thesymbolism.com.

Talmadge, Candace and Simons, Jana (2015) *The Afterlife Healing Circle: How Anyone Can Contact the Other Side.* New Jersey: New Page Books.

Tay, Ian (2022) *Eternity.* Australia: ianchtay@gmail.com.

Taylor, Sandra Anne (2016) *The Akashic Records: Unlock the Infinite Power, Wisdom, and Energy of the Universe.* Carlsbad (CA): Hay House Basics.

Teja, Sai (2021) 'Quantum Theory – A Theory Which Completely Changed Our Understanding'. *AtomsTalk*: http://atomstalk.com.

Thomas, Gary (1991) *The Australian Aborigines in Education: A Conflict of Cultures.* Brisbane: The University of Queensland, Aboriginal and Torres Strait Islander Unit.

Tolle, Eckhart (1997) *The Power of Now: A Guide to Spiritual Enlightenment*. Novato (CA): New World Library.
Tolle, Eckhart (2005) *A New Earth: Awakening to Your Life's Purpose*. London: Viking Press.
Unionpedia Communication: The Concept Map (2022) 'James Booth (Mathematician)'. https://en.unionpedia.org.
Valadian, Margaret (1991) *Aboriginal Education - Development or Destruction: The Issues and Challenges That Have to be Recognised*. Armidale: University of New England.
Van Auken, John (2014) *Edgar Cayce on the Spiritual Forces Within You: Unlock Your Soul with Dreams, Intuition, Kundalini and Meditation*. Virginia Beach (VA): A.R.E. Press.
Van Eyk McCain, Marian (2004) *The Lilypad List: Seven Steps to the Simple Life*. Forres (Scotland): Findhorn Press.
Van Praagh, James (1999) *Reaching to Heaven: A Spiritual Journey Through Life and Death*. New York: Signet.
Van Praagh, James (2001) *Heaven and Earth: Making the Psychic Connection*. New York: Simon & Schuster.
Van Praagh, James (2014) *Adventures of the Soul: Journeys Through the Physical and Spiritual Dimensions*. Carlsbad (CA): Hay House.
Van Praagh, James (2016) *The Power of Love: Connecting to the Oneness*. Carlsbad (CA): Hay House.
Van Praagh, James (2017) *Wisdom From Your Spirit Guides: A Handbook to Contact Your Soul's Greatest Teachers*. Carlsbad (CA): Hay House.
Virtue, Doreen (2007) *How to Hear Your Angels*. Carlsbad (CA): Hay House.
Virtue, Doreen (2009) *Signs From Above: Your Angel's Messages About Your Life Purpose*. Carlsbad (CA): Hay House.
Voigt, Anna and Drury, Neville (1997) *Wisdom From the Earth: The Living Legacy of the Aboriginal Dreamtime*. Sydney: Simon & Schuster.
The Wachowskis (Directors) (1999) *The Matrix*. United States of America: Warner Bros. et al.
Wachowski, Lana (Dir.) (2021) *The Matrix Resurrections*. United States of America: Warner Bros. Pictures et al.
Wassmann, Jurg (1998) *Pacific Answers to Western Hegemony: Cultural Practices of Identity Construction*. Oxford: Berg.

Watts, Quentin and Canisius, Vicki (1994) *Dreams: Signs of Things to Come*. Sydney: ABC Books.

Way, Bruce (1998) *How to Interpret a Psychic Reading*. Melbourne: Lothian Books.

Weiten, Wayne (1998) *Psychology: Themes and Variations*. Pacific Grove (CA): Brooks / Cole Publishing Company.

White, Gloria (2022) 'Infinity Symbol: Origins, Meaning, and Spiritual Significance'. https://thefifthelementlife.com.

Wikipedia (2022) 'Infinity', 'Quantum Mechanics', 'Old Quantum Theory', 'Many-Worlds Interpretation', 'Ouroboros', 'Anaximander', 'Apeiron', 'Shukarahasya Upanishad', 'Nature Worship' ('Naturalistic Pantheism', 'Panentheism', 'Totemism', 'Animism'), 'Celtic Paganism', 'Shinto', and 'Rupert Sheldrake'. http://en.wikipedia.org.

Williams, Lisa (2018) *Divine Wisdom: Messages of Love, Hope, and Healing from the Masters*. Lismore: Animal Dreaming Publishing.

Willis, Jim (2019) *The Quantum Akashic Field: A Guide to Out-of-Body Experiences for the Astral Traveller*. Rochester (VA): Findhorn Press.

Wilson Schaef, Anne (1995) *Native Wisdom for White Minds: Daily Reflections Inspired by the Native Peoples of the World*. London: One World.

Wolf, Fred Alan (1989) *Taking the Quantum Leap: The New Physics for Non-scientists*. New York: Harper Perennial.

Yunkaporta, Tyson (2019) *Sand Talk: How Indigenous Thinking Can Save the World*. Melbourne: Text Publishing.

Zukav, Gary (1990) *The Seat of the Soul: An Inspiring Vision of Humanity's Spiritual Destiny*. London: Rider.

Recommended Films, Documentaries, and Television Series

Brand, Joshua and Falsey, John (Creators) (1990-1995) *Northern Exposure* (Seasons 1-6). USA: CineNevada Productions et al.

Caro, Niki (Dir.) (2003) *Whale Rider.* New Zealand: South Pacific Pictures et al.

Costner, Kevin (Dir.) (1990) *Dances With Wolves.* United States of America: Tig Productions.

de Heer, Rolf and Djigirr, Peter (Directors) (2006) *Ten Canoes.* Australia: Adelaide Film Festival et al.

Erlingsson, Benedikt (Dir.) (2018) *Woman at War.* Iceland: Slot Machine et al.

Gibson, Dean (Dir.) (2021) *Incarceration Nation.* Australia: Bent3Land Productions.

Guggenheim, Davis (Dir.) (2006) *An Inconvenient Truth.* United States of America: Lawrence Bender Productions et al.

Haynes, Todd (Dir.) (2019) *Dark Waters.* USA: Participant et al.

Hogan, Melanie (Dir.) (2006) *Kanyini.* Australia: Bob Randall et al.

Kay, Jeff et al (Directors) (2015-2022) *Alone.* United States of America: Leftfield Pictures.

Ma, Nicole (Dir.) (2015) *Putuparri and the Rainmakers.* Australia: Ronin Films et al.

Moore, Michael (Dir.) (2015) *Where to Invade Next.* United States of America: Dog Eat Dog Films et al.

Noyce, Phillip (Dir.) (2002) *Rabbit-Proof Fence.* Australia: Rumbalara Films et al.

Penn, Sean (Dir.) (2007) *Into the Wild.* United States of America: Paramount Vantage et al.

Permezel, Bruce and Skirving, Rhian (Directors) (2022) *Greenhouse by Joost.* Australia: GoodThing Productions.

Shearman, Stephen et al (Directors) (2006-2011) *Man vs Wild / Born Survivor* (Seasons 1-7). United Kingdom: Diverse Productions.

Vallee, Jean-Marc (Dir.) (2014) *Wild.* United States of America: Pacific Standard et al.

Williams, Paul Damien (Dir.) (2018) *Gurrumul.* Australia: 6 Seasons Productions et al.

Winkler, Irwin (Dir.) (2001) *Life as a House.* United States of America: Winkler Films.

Zaillian, Steven (Dir.) (1998) *A Civil Action.* United States of America: Touchstone Pictures et al.

www.ingramcontent.com/pod-product-compliance
Lightning Source LLC
Chambersburg PA
CBHW040306170426
43194CB00022B/2916